ADDICTED
NO MORE

Jason Miller

Addicted No More

Cover Design: Reddovedesign.com

Interior Design: Reddovedesign.com

ISBN-13: 978-0997769135 (Red Dove Publishing)

ISBN-10: 0997769130

Printed in the United States of America

DEDICATION

I want to dedicate this book to all those who are at home, jails, prisons, programs, institutions, that have not given up on the hope that it is possible to experience being Addicted No More.

PREFACE

It has been a long road for me. To be at this place in my life—happily married, sober, helping others to find freedom from their addictions as a counselor, and seeing this book completed—is just amazing miracle. My parents split up when I was just seven years old and by the time I was thirteen had been sexually abused by four different older men. Dealt with these situations by getting high. Smoked, huffed, snorted, swallowed, drank and injected drugs with a needle starting at age ten and continued this behavior for twenty years. It led to plenty of jail time. Was locked up for a total of five years in programs, jails, and prison. Racking up thirteen felonies, mostly from theft to keep my habit going, robbed dope dealers, banks, stores, homes, cars, and people. If that wasn't enough, injuries forced me to have two back surgeries which led to ten years of opiate pain pill addiction. Incredibly, was struck by lighting and had 50% of my body burned! My life was full of pain and trouble, but after two marriages, being a deadbeat dad, and empty spiritually, found healing in a deep personal relationship with Jesus Christ, who rebuilt my relationships, helped me love myself again, found permanent inner healing, and lifelong sobriety with love, joy, peace, and happiness.

My purpose of writing this book was because deep down inside felt there were many pathways to sobriety, but only one way for each person. Spent many years in and out of what I thought might work for me.

Found out that in all my studies of addiction that 90% of those living in sobriety and peace in all areas of life are working a *daily* spiritual program. There are only a select few who are committed to their sobriety, like I was to my dope. I realized that if I wanted true freedom I had to go after my recovery like I did my alcohol and drugs. Needed them daily. My dream is to get this message across to those who continue to struggle, so they can be set free, too. Wrote this book to teach you how to approach recovery in that same way. If I did not have my dope daily I was sick. The path to recovery must be no different. My desire is for you to find hope in my story; that what I have to say will help you to "get after it" daily and truly be Addicted No More.

ACKNOWLEDGEMENTS

I want to thank my Mother and Father who went to bed many nights wondering if I was going to be dead or alive when they woke up in the morning. You are both my friends and mentors and greatest supporters. Thanks for never giving up on your son. Thank you to my beautiful wife, who is both my friend and biggest fan, for always supporting me, and pushing me to follow my dreams. Thank you to Overcomers Living Free and the teachings of David Cox who taught me what it meant to have a two-way conversation with God through journaling and for walking me through my own personal Inner Healing. Thank you to Brother Rick Aanonsen who taught me how to align my 'hips with my lips.' And I want to thank New Life Christian Fellowship and East Coast Christian Center/University for laying the foundation for the truth concerning the Holy Spirit, which is the key ingredient to true lifelong sobriety.

TABLE OF CONTENTS

BOOK

WORKBOOK

PART ONE

ONE

Addicted No More

BOOK

chapter one

THE ENCOUNTER OF A LIFETIME

As we venture into my story, it will be important for you to be open to some things that you may have never heard before. I am very transparent and a "keeping it real" type of guy. I want to share my personal experience of abuse, rejection, drugs, and the darkness that it brought me into the loneliest place I have ever been on this earth. These many years of undealt with emotions and the empty void inside seemed to continually burn a hole through my soul.

When I was eighteen years old, I accelerated my life of crime.

I was arrested and locked up for armed robbery with a fire arm. A friend and I came up with the perfect crime, one we thought no one would never go to jail for--robbing drug dealers! Let's face it, what drug dealer would ever call the cops and say, "I was robbed; some guys stole my drugs and my money." And this is what we told ourselves as we carefully planned each robbery. It was foolproof.

Although we only pulled a few of them, this is how we did it on this particular robbery. I found this drug dealer and started buying small amounts of weed from him to build his trust. Every time I showed up to buy the stuff, I would scan the house and surroundings, checking the layout of things, and then tell my buddies what to expect. Things looked good, so I set up a buy for one pound of weed, and went inside the dealer's house to check the quality. After checking the quality, I told the dealer I would be back with the cash. I walked out and met up with my two friends back at the car, and sent them in to do the robbery. My job was to set up the deal, provide the gun and do the driving.

When my friends went in, it got bloody! The dealer was not willing to just lay down and get ripped off. No shots were fired, but he received a pretty bad beating—well he did have a wallet full of money as well as a pound of dope!

This must all seem hardcore, but so many of us do such things in an attempt to deal with unbearable pain, with buried emotions and to fill the incredible void inside. The extent of the hurt, pain and depth of the void determine the types of crazy things we do. Ok, not many of us go to the extremes as I did, but the thoughts we entertain about what we could do to others would result in you being locked up just like me.

So, after we were all were bruised and bloodied, you will never guess what happened next! Yes, the drug dealer called the cops!

We ran off in three different directions but I was the only one arrested and charged with armed robbery with a deadly weapon. While in jail, the State Attorney's best offer to me was seven to ten years minimum mandatory, and if I went to trial and lost I would get twenty-five years to life in prison. Up to this point I had already been locked up several times, tried as an adult, and had been in three rehab programs for troubled teens. In the court's eyes, it was not looking good for me. So, like most of us when we are in deep trouble or distress, I started calling out to God, not even knowing if there was a God. As a kid, I had remembered going to church a couple of times with my brothers. I was around seven or eight years old when I had been water baptized. That is all I really remember about church or God.

I was thrown into the Orange County Jail in Orlando, FL, which was on the fourth floor of the Horizon building. That's when I started praying every night, "God, if you are real please show yourself to me and help me." I did this every single night before going to bed for a couple of months. There was this one night I really struggled and I just could not go to sleep. I was consumed with the emotions I had bottled up for so long and the empty void burning and tormenting the inside of me. I began replaying my life, the last couple of years, being locked up or in a program, and the thought of going to prison for what could be twenty-five years was unbearable. I was appointed a lawyer from the state who said that because there were three people involved in the crime yet only I had been arrested, I might have a chance at a lighter sentence. If we were to lose, however, I'd get the max of twenty-five years. I was in deep torment. What had my life become? I was a hot mess. That's when I experienced something supernatural.

I was awake in bed and had pulled the covers up over my head. I was miserable. I just lay there, under the blanket, with my eyes wide open. That's when I saw something incredible. It was a ball of light floating in the middle of my jail cell room. Inside this ball of light was what seemed to be a brick wall with people standing on the other side of the wall. They were waiving and moving their hands and speaking, but I could not hear or understand what they were saying or doing, but I felt a strange sense that this was from God. The light was so powerful that I could not move, it was like I was pinned to the bed by the force of what seemed to be a powerful presence. I tried to speak out loud to say, "God, is this you?" But I couldn't utter a word; my mouth was frozen shut due to this powerful presence. In my mind I said, "God is this you?" and what seemed like an audible voice answered, "Believe in Me and My Son, Jesus, and I will show you what this all means."

This was my first experience and encounter with God. Up until this time I had no proof that God existed, and even if He did, which God was the right God? Allah, Buddha, Krishna, Jesus? Yet, God in His great love and kindness saw that my heart and motives for asking Him to reveal Himself to me were pure. He heard my deep crying out for truth, showed me that the God of Jesus, the God of the Bible was who I was to believe.

Another amazing thing happened with this experience. While all this was taking place, the void that ate at me day after day vanished. I had no emptiness inside during this vision. I felt fully complete.

While waiting to go to trial I started reading my Bible and began attending all the church programs available to me in jail, I even started a Bible study myself. I would ask God in little prayers and He would answer them. One time I ask God to let my dad come and visit me and the next day my dad showed up for a visit! He told me he had awakened that morning with a very strong desire to visit me. God had actually become very real to me through all this and although I can't make God real for you, what I can tell you is that God is no respecter of persons. I am fully convinced that if anyone on the earth asked God, and really wanted to know, asking Him with a pure heart and pure motives for Him to reveal Himself, He would do it.

So, what is there to lose? I can't say that He will reveal Himself the same way he did with me. I am a bit hardheaded and He knew that without real proof I would not believe. He could send someone to talk to you and that might be enough for you. But He will make Himself real to you, if you ask. Call it what you may, but I call it a God loving His children so much that if we call out to Him He will stop Heaven and earth for us.

I was able to get into the Christian pod that Good News Jail offered at the jail. Getting placed in this cell block kept you safe from harm and offered Bible studies, meetings, worship and only Christians who underwent and passed the interview process were transferred there. I did Bible correspondence courses and learned a lot while waiting to go to trial.

Then God sent another sign. My mom sent me a book called "Piercing the Darkness" by Frank Peretti. My lawyer advised me that we should take my case to trial because of the lack of evidence the state had against me. When it was time for me to go to trial, I was scared because I knew deep down I was guilty and so I asked God for a sign that all would end well. On the first day of trial, one of the jurors was carrying the same book my mother gave me, "Piercing the Darkness." I was amazed! You see, God loves our child-like faith and knows exactly what we need when we need it. When the trial had finally ended, to my surprise, I was found not guilty, not only on one charge but on all charges against me and I was free. Another miracle had happened!

How I would love to tell you that I went on to live this perfect life with no more problems after this encounter and this miracle that just happened! Most of you reading this know that seldom happens in life. You have probably met someone that was radically set free, finds God, and then goes on to live a great life helping others, but my experience shows that this does not happen often.

You see, I had an awesome experience where the Creator of Heaven and earth saw my heart and heard my cry, and out of His great love for me, revealed Himself to me. I had learned and saw for myself that an experience without a relationship is just that, an experience. I still had an ongoing relationship with my undealt with emotions, my drugs, and my own attempts to fill the empty void that lingered on inside of me.

chapter two

OUT OF JAIL AND BACK IN

When I got out of jail, I was fully convinced that I was set free, full of Jesus, never going back to my old ways again. But, because I had no real one-on-one relationship with God. He was just a seed in my heart. I did not yet understand that I still had many years of unresolved hurt and pain, and that I had to get my love, joy, peace, and happiness through a daily one-on-one relationship with God. Deep down I could relate to this kind of relationship, because I had to meet with my drugs two to three times a day to stay happy and to keep from getting sick.

So, because of the cares of the world and the pleasures of life, my need for God was gone very quickly. I was still somewhat sober in my eyes because I was not using street drugs, but I filled my heart with the lies of what the American culture and the world system called success and happiness. From our early years in school we are taught to get an education, a successful job, and a happy family. We must work hard to provide for our loved ones and only after years and years of this can we retire, sit back, and enjoy our store house of money, and relax. This, in a nut shell, is what many of us like to call, "Living the American Dream."

Jesus said it like this in Luke 12:13-21 NIV:

> "[13] Someone in the crowd said to Him, 'Teacher, tell my brother to divide the family inheritance with me.' [14] But He said to him, 'Man, who appointed Me a judge or arbitrator

over you?' [15] Then He said to them, 'Beware, and be on your guard against every form of greed; for not even when one has an abundance does his life consist of his possessions.' [16] And He told them a parable, saying, 'The land of a rich man was very productive.' [17] And he began reasoning to himself, saying, 'What shall I do, since I have no place to store my crops?' [18] Then he said, 'This is what I will do: I will tear down my barns and build larger ones, and there I will store all my grain and my goods.' [19] And I will say to my soul, 'Soul, you have many goods laid up for many years to come; take your ease, eat, drink and be merry.' [20] But God said to him, 'You fool! This very night your soul is required of you; and now who will own what you have prepared?' [21] So is the man who stores up treasure for himself, and is not rich toward God."

Jesus throws a bit of a "monkey wrench" in the American dream picture. Notice in verse 19, the rich guy says to his soul (mind, will and emotions), "Soul, you have many goods laid up for many years to come; take your ease, eat, drink and be merry." If Jesus was living His earthly life today He would be talking to many of us reading this book, the addicted and the afflicted.

It might amaze you to know that if you make $10,000 or more per year you are wealthier than 80% of the world's population. If you make $40,000 or more a year, you are part of the top 1% of the world's wealthiest. Which means you and I are considered filthy rich compared to most people in the world. Most of us have had the house, car, husband/wife, job, children, grandchildren, boat, motorcycle, and it's still not enough because we are addicted and afflicted. None of this brings happiness if we have unresolved emotions, let alone the stress of dealing with our day-to-day emotions. We must get our love, joy, peace and happiness from the One who created us and that can only be found in a true one-on-one relationship with God himself.

Within six months of being free, I had wrecked my truck, lost my girlfriend and went back to the old friends that I used to hang with. Out of loneliness, with no job and no girl, I started partying again and it wasn't long until I landed back in jail again. This time around it was for robbing houses. I was with a couple of friends and we robbed houses from Florida all the way to Missouri. When we were busted in Arkansas, the police caught us with guns and pillow cases full of jewelry, cameras, video games and other electronics. While in the county jail waiting for all the charges to pile up, I felt so confused. I had just spent a year in jail, went to trial, was set free and then six months later was locked up again. "Why?" I said, "How did I get to this point so quickly?"

I remember being so desperate that I even said to Satan in my heart, "If you let me break out of this jail then I will be with you." Within seconds of thinking this, I repented and asked God to forgive me for saying such a thing. I remember it like it was yesterday. I have never shared this with anyone. It is not something I am proud of; it is the first and only time I have ever asked or considered anything from Satan—I didn't even know much about him other than what I had read in the Bible.

You see, I had a one-time experience with God so He could prove to me that He was real and on my side. But without a relationship, no real change was ever going to happen.

We were all sentenced to prison and then had to travel to Missouri to face charges there. The State of Missouri ran their charges concurrent with Arkansas, and prison was our destination. While in prison, I was put in a different building from those I got in trouble with and could get reconnected with God. I started going to chapel, Bible study and became close with the chaplain. I then grew in great knowledge of things concerning the Bible and church tasks. I helped where I could. I was writing letters to my family about how Jesus had changed my life and that things were going to be different.

I turned twenty-one years old while in prison. I was sent back to Florida to face violation of probation for charges against me when I was tried as an adult at fifteen years of age. I remember that they flew me in a small airplane with six other men like me, with no parachutes, and all handcuffed to each other. It was some wild trip!

I was able to get into the Christian cell in the Seminole County Jail with Good News Jail just as I had been in Orange County Jail. After a few months, I was able to go to court and was sentenced to two years' house arrest with five years of probation.

I got out of prison and came home to my mother's house. I read my Bible every morning and every night. Mom and I started going to a great Methodist church that we loved. She and I often talk about how much we loved that church. This time I was fully convinced I had it all figured out. I was still planning my life to get my love, joy, peace, and happiness. My plan was to get a job, get a car, and find a wife and a home. The American Dream, right? If you get all these things, plus God, then you are golden. Everything is well, your name is written in Heaven. You live Heaven on earth to retire, relax, and then go to your mansion in Heaven.

I was able to find a good job, and then I met a girl at work. She was giving me the eye and of course I was doing the same. We started to date and hang out, and even started to read the Bible together. However, we were getting involved sexually and within a few weeks she invited me to play pool at a bar. I was offered weed and alcohol. Of course, I knew smoking weed was out of the question because of the house arrest, but I did not want ruin the party so I had a few beers. The house arrest officer told me that he was okay with whatever I did if I was home by 10 pm. Well, the Bible reading and going to church soon stopped and within a couple of months my girlfriend became pregnant. I wanted to do the right thing, so we got married and started our life, or so I thought.

I acquired a good job with a great company and we moved into our own place. It was not long before we started drinking daily. While working, I hurt my back and started taking prescribed pain killers per doctor's orders. The back pain was so bad I ended up having back surgery and was not able to work for almost a year. Neither of us were satisfied with our relationship and during this time we both decided to call it quits. We divorced and she left with my daughter. We had been together for four years and all during this time I had pushed God out of my life and because of the divorce I lost my daily relationship with my daughter.

I had just two months left on my probation and was alone in my home by myself. I was working for a friend who smoked weed every day along with many other drugs. I worked a light duty job at the time and I was not doing anything illegal, but the alcohol and pain pills I was prescribed were my legal addiction. I was deceived in my own mind because the pain killers were doctor ordered, and of course I was taking the pain killers big time. Seven to ten a day! Since alcohol was legal and I was paying my bills I told myself, "You are doing great, you are ready for this!"

Probation ended and the very next day in my friend's truck, I smoked weed. Although I knew about God, I did not know Him. I kept hearing the lies in my mind screaming at me, "You are a loser; you failed your marriage, you lost your daughter, you lost everything and now you're getting high again." This only added to the twenty years of undealt with issues that I still carried around inside of me.

In reality, when I drank that beer after I got out of prison it was all over. While on probation I went many years without doing drugs of any kind, because I could suppress my emotions with a limited supply of substances. I could do it then because my greatest desire was never going back to prison! But when the thumb of the law was not holding me back, I was all in. I just wanted to stop hurting, stop feeling alone, and stop feeling like a loser. I felt so shameful after smoking weed for the first time. It hurt so bad I wanted to cry. I really thought that maybe this was my lot in life. The shame and guilt of my present, past and future were so powerful I went into full-blown addiction. My life revolved around parties, selling drugs and using anything to keep the voices from speaking the truth about who I was, but in reality, they were all lies.

Those voices started when I was a young boy, just ten years old. I was sexually abused from ten to twelve years of age; I started to believe the lies that came from deep within that abuse. I continued to replay them in my head which kept me bound up in misery. I had hundreds of thoughts about this abuse that I continued to feed on and replay over and over again. They only came back to my mind when I was sober. So, to fight it off, I stayed high.

Life just got worse for me. I became involved with old friends again. We started to get into music, doing turn tables and were called the Florida Break Beats. During this time I continued the use of my prescription pain medication from the doctor. The back surgery had not been successful, and the pain in my back was unbearable at times. I couldn't ease the torture, even with overdoing it on the meds.

One day the pain in my back was so bad one of my friends said, "Sniff this and your back will not hurt." He was right. This is how I was introduced to heroin. This friend is now dead due to heroin overdose. RIP Robbie Brown. I was hooked! I started doing coke, ecstasy, ketamine, GHP, crack, weed, alcohol, and pain pills. Within a couple of months, I was doing all of these sometimes in the same day, and began selling them as well to support my main addiction, which was now heroin and cocaine.

You see, the drugs worked for me all the time, they never let me down. I had a one-on-one relationship with them. I spent time with them and learned the best ways to do them and they always took the hurt, the pain, and the shame away.

In the midst of my addiction, I met my second wife, someone who had never done street drugs like me. Although she only drank, I soon found out that she was selling weed. She connected me to a big ecstasy dealer and my drug involvement skyrocketed! At one point I was getting five hundred to one thousand pills of ecstasy at a time. My life now had now revolved around drug dealing and party hopping. I became a non-stop train, reeling out of control. I was doing massive amounts of ecstasy, cocaine and heroin. Up to this point I had been snorting and smoking the drugs but after shooting up with a needle, the high came so much quicker, it worked within seconds of injecting it. Out of all the drugs I abused, it was heroin that made me feel the most complete in my emotions and filled my empty void. When my wife found out what I was doing she said she had to try this heroin to understand why I could not quit. She tried it and she became addicted! She started slow, only doing it a couple of times a week instead of a couple times a day like I did. She and I started pulling away from the crowd because that is what you do when you are addicted. At first you are with friends and it is all social fun and then you think to yourself, "I need all I can get for me."

It wasn't long until we both began shooting cocaine and heroin regularly. It was a slow descent into a very dark and empty world. Heroin by itself keeps you medicated and somewhat alert but unresponsive. But cocaine and crack take you into a dirty world where you're chasing the devil himself. Just thinking and writing about the despair and the loneliness that overtakes you when you come down from cocaine gives me a knot in my stomach. I can only compare it to what I think hell might be like. Yes, I do believe in hell, and I believe there is a deep dark evil in the world that is out to kill you and me. Because I have lived it and it is no joke. Once you are hooked in this lifestyle, the chances of getting out are slim to none.

God was still on my radar during these times, but up until this point in my life my knowledge of Him came through what I had read in the Bible and a one-time vision experience.

Let me give you an example of how that may play out in a husband and wife relationship. Let's say I met a girl who would become my wife and one night we go out and have a great time and fall in puppy love. Later on, I send her a few emails, asking her for things. I then just talk to her every once in a while, when I have problems or get in trouble. I drive by and see her house, but I don't talk to her for years at a time. That's how it was with me and my relationship with God. If I had real relationship with my wife and I truly loved, honored and valued her, I'd be talking to her and, more importantly, listening to her, spending time with her, laughing and crying, and just enjoying each other in silence. God wants the same type of relationship with you and me.

In the parable of the soil and seed in Luke 8:14:

"The seeds that fell among the thorns represent those who hear the message, but all too quickly the message is crowded out by the cares and riches and pleasures of this life. And so they never grow into maturity."

I had heard the truth before, but it was just knowledge, so it was stolen from me every time. No one had ever shared a one-on-one relationship with me where I had to go deeper than my relationship with drugs, and because drugs supply a certain 'feel good' feeling, I am convinced that only a one-on-one relationship with God, where His presence jacks you up more than your addiction of choice, will keep you from going back to the destructive relationship of drugs.

Rules and religion and a forty-five minute sermon on Sunday will never work for people like you and me. We need a God to whom we can have full access. We need to know how to access His power and presence so we can get jacked-up on Him, instead of with the needle shooting of cocaine and heroin.

Please understand, I am not using God to get high, but those who are addicted like I was can relate to what I am talking about. If we can't find this type of encounter in Christ, then we will go back to our drugs every time. By my own experience in this process, I can assure you we do have access to God 24/7. All the feelings that drugs, alcohol, pain pills, and life controlling behaviors give you are counterfeits of God's awesome power and presence. There is a way out and we are going to walk this journey of freedom together!

chapter three

LIGHTNING SHOULD CHANGE YOU

On the morning of July 17, 2001, I found myself in a dead-end life-style of shooting heroin, cocaine, and smoking crack. I was doing this daily. I was in a misery of deep darkness, desperately wanting things to change. That morning I had run out of heroin to shoot up, so I was super sick. As I was getting ready to leave for work, I looked at my wife and then looked up into the sky and said out loud, "God, I don't want to live like this anymore; do whatever you have to do to get my life right."

I headed to work feeling really sick from withdrawals. It was five hours later when something incredibly weird happened. With the sun shining and not a cloud in the sky, I was struck by lightning! The lightning came through the roof of a building I was working on at the time. I was on a six-foot ladder putting up metal hurricane straps with an air powered palm nail gun. The apartment building construction site had a twenty car garage and I was working there when the lightning came through the roof and into my head. I can't recall anything about being struck by the lightning; one minute I was on the ladder and the next thing I remember was wide awake, lying on the ground, flat on my back.

As I came to my senses I notice a pool of blood coming from my head and smoke coming off of my body. When I tilted my head up off the ground to look at my body I was confused about what was going on; it felt like I was bathing in a pool of fire. As I looked at my body I noticed ashes on each side of me. My shirt was gone and had turned in to ashes as I saw it lying beside me. When I looked at my skin it looked to be melted, and just like red meat. I vaguely remember someone trying to move me and saying to them, "Please, just let me lie down..." I don't recall being able to move at all, but I do remember the pain I was experiencing.

The next thing I knew I was in the hospital and my family was visiting me. The doctors didn't think I was going to live through this. In my mind I kept wishing they would just hurry up and sedate me so the pain would stop. I was in so much pain and kept going in and out of consciousness. I would hear only a piece of a conversation here or there. It's funny, the last thing I remember was two guys talking about some girls as they were putting staples in my head from the injury that happened when I fell off the six-foot ladder. Thirty days later I woke up, still in the hospital. When I woke up the words that I said out loud to God came back to me: "I don't want to live like this anymore, do whatever you have to do to get my life right."

My family told me that my face and body were so swollen that I was unrecognizable. The doctors said the pain medicine wasn't helping, and if they could not stabilize me, the shock from the burns would kill me. My full chest, back, parts of one arm and a quarter of my left leg had third degree burns. My older brother realized why they could not stabilize me with the pain medication: it was due to my tolerance to it from shooting heroin. He explained this to the doctors. Up to this point they had given me enough morphine to kill several people. It all made sense to them now. They found a way, somehow, to stabilize me and I was put into an induced coma for thirty days while they worked with the burns and skin grafts.

I have very little memory of the first month or even after I woke up from the coma and recovered somewhat in the hospital. I was on so much medication that most of it was a blur. I am thankful that it was this way, because the pain was too tough to bear.

In the beginning, after this horrible accident first happened, I truly thought that God Himself sent a bolt of lightning out of Heaven to fix me. I always had that picture of God in my mind—that if you did something wrong or you were not living right, He would make you pay for it. Over the years, I have matured in God and have received personal revelation from the Word of God and Jesus Himself. He revealed to me that we are speaking spirits and that our words are very powerful; so powerful in fact, that God has spoken everything into existence with His own words. The Word also reveals to us that death and the life are in the power of the tongue, as Proverbs 18:21 ISV states:

> "The power of the tongue is life and death— those who love to talk will eat what it produces."

I believe the enemy himself heard those words and used them to cause harm on me. But God, in all His mercy, like He did with Job, did not allow the enemy to kill me. God chose to allow it for my greater good, and I am fully convinced had this not happened, I would not be writing this book and would not be sober nor alive.

chapter four

TRUE DARKNESS

I would really love to tell you that I got out of the hospital healed and walked with Jesus all the days of my life since. But, that would be a lie. Things got even worse.

While in the hospital my older brother gratefully looked out for me and found a lawyer. I am so thankful for him for doing this for me. Workman's Comp covered all of my expenses while in the hospital and after I came home the lawyer was able to settle my case with what they called an "act of God."

When they released me from the hospital, I had a mass of pain killers, psychotic drugs and more. I came home with burns and open wounds; dressings that needed to be changed twice a day. Not only did I have to deal with the burns, but in order to get the skin for grafts they used a tool that looked like a cheese grater to cut the skin off around both my legs and from my crotch area down to my knees. As bad as the burns hurt, this hurt just as much, if not more. I was a complete mass of raw skin! I don't think there was a place on my body free from pain. My wife at the time was so very kind to take care of me daily, changing my bandages twice a day. This was a two to three hour process each time.

Now back at home with all the pain medications and being in the same neighborhood, word got out that I was home. People started wanting drugs from me, and in a matter of time I was off to the races again. Only this time I had money coming from worker's comp, pre-scribed pain medication of all sorts, and pills that I didn't want that others bought. Using that money I bought more heroin, cocaine and crack, just picking up where I left off. Sadly, this is the way it happens and it only gets worse; the pit grows even deeper. You see, I had no change, just another experience where God in His mercy saw fit to save me for a greater purpose.

My wife and I lived like this until the lawyer was able to come to an agreement. Part of the agreement was a cash settlement of $100,000. I took the check to the bank, cashed it all, and brought the cash home and hid it in the washer with the dirty clothes. I was doing so much heroin and cocaine, I became paranoid. Things spiraled out of control. With all that money available, we went on a $60,000 drug binge (just writing about it gives me knots on my stomach). Each day we were buying $500 to $1000 "cookies of crack," which are about the size of a small dinner plate. We were shooting so much powdered cocaine and heroin that both of us fell into a drug induced coma. We had overdosed so many times that we had salt water shot into our veins to keep us alive. One time I remember doing such a big hit of cocaine with a needle that I sat on the edge of the couch for what seemed like an hour, shaking and trembling, my heart beating out of my chest. I knew, after this, that if we didn't do something to change we were both going to die.

We decided to pick a place on the map and move so we could get away from all this and get straight. We found a home in Georgia about three hours from Orlando and put a down payment on a house with the arrangement that our rent would be payment towards the purchase of the house. After a few weeks in Georgia, our old drug dealer wanted to come and see us. He offered to give us a really good deal on our dope. At the time, we were doing a gram a day of heroin, along with cocaine, crack and pain killers. We were driving every week to Orlando because we had no connections in Georgia. We would get seven grams of her-oin, cocaine and crack and we would smoke it on the way back home while driving. Within a few months the rest of the money we had left over from the settlement was gone due to buying drugs every week. However, I still had some monthly payments coming in from the settlement. My lawyer said if I took the money up front it would be gone in a year. He was so right.

One day I decided to fry some potatoes for lunch. I turned the stove on and put oil in the pan. Next thing I knew, I woke up with a big cloud of smoke coming from the kitchen, and the walls were black from the smoke. I had gotten so high that day that I passed out after I put the oil in the pan. The landlord saw the damage, kicked us out, and did not return the $27,000 down payment. We had bought a trailer at one time as a rental property and had never rented it, so we had to move there.

When we got our monthly check we would go to Orlando and get our drugs. The money did not last long, so we did what we had to do to get high. We robbed thrift stores and stole merchandise from department stores and returned it for cash. We robbed whoever and whatever we needed to get our drugs. Our weekly trips to Orlando were getting expensive. So one day I pulled up to a sketchy looking apartment building not too far from where we lived and asked for crack and found it.

I have vivid memories of many things in this very dark world of shooting crack and cocaine, which were now our drugs of choice because we no longer had access or a connection for the dirty brown (heroin). We started putting crack in lemon juice to break it down and shooting it in our veins daily. We had so many holes, marks and bruises on our bodies from shooting up that we were forced to wear long sleeved shirts, no matter the weather. When you shoot cocaine it burns your veins and collapses them so you can't shoot into them anymore.

One night both of us were in separate bathrooms trying to shoot up. We were there for hours, desperate to find a vein to use and could not. We would scream out in disappointment every time we missed the vein because it was very painful. I recall walking into the bathroom were my wife was, her arm covered in blood from what looked like a hundred needles marks. I will never forget the deep despair and hopelessness I felt towards her and myself. When I met her she had never done street drugs or even tried them.

We both quit shooting soon after that, not because we wanted to, but because we could not find a viable vein or place to shoot in our bodies. Even though it has many years since I have touched a needle, I still have needle head scars on my hands and arms from trying so hard to dig in and find a vein. With no other alternative, we decided to start smoking crack instead, and when we could get heroin, we would snort it along with prescribed morphine pills, methadone pills, alcohol and Xanax from the doctor.

chapter five

TIME FOR CHANGE

Most of us change in gradual ways or after getting so worn out from our destructive lifestyles. We find a program or diet, and then the change, like walking down a road, slowly puts distance between us and the past. My road was always a dead end, or at best an endless loop, going around and around with no way out. But not on this day.

I needed to refill my prescribed Xanax so I headed to the doctor. I popped open the bottle and took a few. The next thing I remember I was laying on my couch with a hospital band around my arm with a blanket over me. Our car was gone, my wife was gone, and the phone had been shut off. I had no money and no painkillers. This was 2003, the first clarity that I had since I started drinking in 1995 when I got out of prison. Days go by and after several attempts to locate my wife making phone calls at a neighbor's house to locate her; calling hospitals and the jail to see if she was there; and with no substances of any kind I could abuse, I came to my senses in a moment of reality. I fell to my knees and cried out to God and asked Him to forgive me for how I had been living. In that minute of brokenness and with a repentant heart, the peace of God came into the room and overwhelmed me like it did back when I was eighteen and had the vision in the Orange County Jail.

I immediately found a Bible that was in my home, put it on my kitchen table and felt free. I found a Christian TV Station and started watching it, and also found a church nearby that had a prison ministry and started attending that church. I still had not heard from my wife and finally concluded that she had left me and was not coming back. At the time, I felt released from my old life and was okay with her absence because I was back with what I knew of God. One experience with God can change you and I was changed. So often it's not enough to keep you, so I started listening to Christian music and watching Christian TV, to surround myself in His peace. I was all in.

I thought back to the lightning strike and how I had spent all the money on drugs. It was time to grow up. About a week and half went by and I got a letter from my wife. She was in jail in Florida. When she came up missing I had called all the jails and hospitals in Georgia, but not in Florida. She wrote me and explained what had happened that day. She said we had decided to pawn the TV and then drive to Orlando to get some drugs. She said I struggled to take the TV in the pawn shop and kept dropping it. As we left the pawn shop, I wouldn't get in the car to go, so she left me because the pawn shop employees thought my behavior was strange and had called the cops. The cops came to arrest me, but after seeing me they realized I was on some serious drugs, so they called an ambulance to come and take me to the hospital where they had my stomach pumped because I had taken too much Xanax. I was kept in the hospital for a few days. The pawn shop employees told the cops what kind of car she had been driving and the Florida cops pulled her over. She confessed to them that she had taken Xanax as well, so they arrested her. When I received this letter from her, I had no money and no car, so I decided to contact her mother—who knew nothing about drugs or what was happening—to please come and get me to Florida so we could go get her out of jail.

We did manage to get her out jail and she came back home. I was staying true to my new life, as best I could. I was taking only prescribed medicine for my back and would have a few beers every once in a while. For me this was a big step from the street drugs. I was walking what I thought was a straighter line and stayed focused by reading my Bible daily, watching Christian TV, listening to Christian radio and attending church. However, my wife was raised Jewish and didn't believe that Jesus was the Messiah. She seemed okay with me reading my Bible, watching Christian TV and going to a Christian church. She still needed to deal with her emotions, so I split my pain medicine with her, but it wasn't enough. She became fully addicted again and for the first time I was able to see what it was like to deal with the afflicted and addicted, even though deep down I was still addicted myself. She was arrested a couple of times during this season, and I bonded her out each time. A new couple moved in the neighborhood right next to our trailer home. The lady was a crack addict and my wife started to hang out with her. The daily situation grew extremely tough for me to deal with.

Finally, we both came to a decision that the best thing for her was to move away and live with some family, out-of-state, in order to get well. I stayed behind and continued to stay connected with the church. I became involved in Kairos Prison Ministries where I met a cool dude name Hal. I still smoked cigarettes and would go out from time to time and shoot pool and have a few beers out of loneliness. From all that I had lived through, I was extremely excited about a new life and a new start. Looking back, the addiction to pain killers, beer, and nicotine was still there. It is nearly an impossible journey to freedom without the proper guidance, and for most people it can become a long process recovering from the addicted lifestyle, especially without the Lord in your life. I am believing that my story will help you bypass the many things I went through and move you speedily into your healing and wholeness.

After a few months living by myself in Georgia, my dad talked me into moving back to Orlando. I am now so thankful for that. So in 2004 I moved back to Florida and continued to stay focused on Christian TV, music and going to all the church functions with my cool Grandma Miller, who is now in Heaven with the Lord. Grandma and I would go to lunch every Sunday after church and have a couple of drinks, and although I was not using drugs, I was still on high doses of pain medication. I had also gotten in touch with some old friends and would go out with them and have a few beers now and again, which for me, I thought, was okay. Well, let me tell you pain medication and alcohol is just like snorting heroin. It was not daily and I felt I was controlling it so I thought everything was fine.

My wife was dealing with her own battles back where she was. We made an effort to stay in contact the first year and then we just lost touch. Years went by and we eventually filed for divorce. I found out much later that she ended up in prison and finally found help through an eighteen-month rehab program, remarried, and had a son. We did end up connecting on Facebook and I was able to ask for her forgiveness for all we went through and wish her the best in life. The path to recovery is one we must walk on our own. Mine was still in progress.

After about a year into my recovery from street drugs, I hooked up with an old friend and went to see my brother DJ at a club. I had a few beers and all was good. I noticed there were a few friends there that I use to party with and buy drugs from. The music was old school breaks, which by itself can get you in the mood to get high. A friend I was with asked me if I wanted cocaine, so I agreed to go in half's on an eight ball and I took the bait. We were all invited then to an after party. I ended up buying five hits of ecstasy at that party—giving my friend one hit and taking the other four for myself. We did about a gram of coke in the bathroom, socializing in-between bumps. My friend came up missing and I went looking for him and found him in the backyard "blowing up" from the ecstasy. "You can have it; I am messed up," he said, handing me the rest of his cocaine to me. I finished the rest of the 8 ball on my own along with 4 hits of ETC and lots of alcohol. I recall vividly how much of a scumbag loser I felt afterwards. I went home and it took me two to three days to fully come off of all that. The misery of coming down off ecstasy and cocaine is the worst feeling of loneliness, with a soul sucking black hole of emptiness that can't be explained or imagined. Death seems like the only way out to escape from it. Only those that have experienced it and have come down off of these drugs know what I am talking about. I made a decision that day that I could not put myself in that environment ever again! I could not be in an environment that would give me access to the people or the music that always drove my soul to a deeper desire to get high. To this day I still cannot listen to rave music of any kind.

I made it through a couple more years living in Orlando before I moved to Titusville, Florida. I had always dreamed of moving back to that town because I remembered having good times in that place as a kid. I found a good church there and became involved in a discipleship course where they introduced me to the gifts of the Spirit. During this time my back pain reached the point where the pain meds were not working and I could barely get around. I knew it was time to search for a doctor for I knew I would need another back surgery.

In 2007, I met my God appointed wife. How God put us together was incredible. We met and married three months later. I had been praying for a few years that God would bless me with a Godly wife. I was specific for what I was looking for in a lady and truly desired a God centered relationship. I knew the path I had gone down before and I didn't want to get hurt-or hurt anyone else by having a relationship outside of God.

A couple of weeks before meeting my future wife, I was watching a teaching message on the Christian channel. Something the guy was saying stood out to me. "If you are believing for something step out in faith! Start putting your plans into motion like you've already received what you're believing for; Buy something..." So I went to a store and bought a gift for my future wife. It was a music box. It had a round glass bowl on the top with a dove inside, representing the Holy Spirit. I found a place to put it in the house where I could see it often and then said, "I will give this to my wife."

I had reminded God often that the Bible said, "It's not good for man to be alone,..." Two weeks later I met my beautiful Colombian bride on-line who lived in the Orlando area just an hour from me. It is amazing to see God give you what you have been praying and stepping out in faith for; when it comes, you know it's from Him.

The instant I met her I knew she was going to be my wife. I was so sure that I gave her the Holy Spirit music box on our second date. I would really love to tell you we stayed holy and kept it between the lines before we got married but that would be a lie. A month after we crossed the line, we sealed it with marriage. We drove to Boone, NC, so she could meet my mom and we got married there. When we got back to Florida just a few days later I had my second back surgery. Not much of a honeymoon! One day I will give her the honeymoon she deserves.

The new doctor assured me that this surgery would fix things and I would never have to take pain pills again. I wanted to have a normal life, be active and lift things again. I had promised my wife I would quit smoking before this surgery and I did! Later, however, for a short time I picked up the habit of dipping snuff. The surgery recovery was as painful as the lightning strike recovery had been. I was in the hospital for a week, screaming in pain.

The surgery was a major one. They laid me open about 10 inches and put screws and rods and other types of stuff in me. It wasn't until about eight to ten months later that I started to feel better and gradually weaned myself off the pain medication. Before the surgery, I was taking lots of pain medication after recovering 8 months later. I tapered myself down on the pain meds. This low dose caused mild withdrawals symptoms so I found another doctor and told him my whole story. I wanted to detox off of my current dose of medication completely. He said it could be done and he'd help me. I came home that day and flushed ALL of my prescribed medication down the toilet—everything that was in the house pertaining to any type of pain killers, as well as other medications. Over a $1000 worth of street value pain medication gone in a second. This was a huge step in my recovery, to actually see all those drugs swirling around and then out of sight. I knew in my mind I could still legally take them or even sell them, but the decision was made; I did not regret it. The withdrawals lasted for a few weeks and I lingered on the couch for about a month, and just like that—cold turkey, I was free from all pain killers.

My wife and I were sold out to Christ. We watched Christian TV together, and went to church and read the Bible together. We still would drink some wine and I would have some beers, but that all came to an end in 2008. My twin brother and I decided to go out to a bar in our old drug town to play pool. We had a couple of beers but it soon got out of hand and I ended up in a very negative scene with him. We were both "cutting the rug" and feeling pretty good about ourselves. There were women coming on to us and although we didn't act upon it, either one of us could've easily been with another woman that night. On the drive home, the Lord really arrested my heart about alcohol. It didn't add any good thing to me but only brought destruction. Even one drink made me cocky with how I spoke to my wife. Since that day in 2008, with the help of the Lord, I have never taken a drink again and my wife made the same decision. God was smart enough to hook me up with a wife that had never used drugs of any kind other than alcohol, and yes, I believe anything that alters your mind is a drug, including alcohol. The sign above ABC liquor stores have it right when it says, "Fine Alcohol & Spirits,"—evil ones, I say.

> Proverbs 31:4 NIV says, "It is not for kings, Lemuel—it is not for kings to drink wine, not for rulers to crave beer."

If He is a king and I belong to the King of all kings, this advice seemed pretty sound. If our Daddy is King then we are King's Kids, so we are Kings ourselves. I had also been thinking strongly at this time in my life that I wanted to help others who struggled with addiction. I felt it was hypocritical of me to lead others out of this lifestyle and still be hooked on a substance of any kind. I needed to be completely free from ALL addictions.

chapter six

TRYING TO MAKE SENSE
OF IT ALL

Today, 2017, I am sober and have been off the needle for fourteen years, nine years free of pain killers, and I haven't consumed alcohol or nicotine for eight. Through these addictive years, I had been searching for the why—the real reason for all the destruction and misery. While being involved in the addiction recovery field I was connected with some great teachings about inner healing, or as some call it, "soul healing" or the healing of our mind, will, and emotions. But it wasn't until I was under some good teaching and had a profound dream about how it all worked that I came into a deep understanding of the soul (our mind, will, and emotions) and the empty void that burns deep in the middle of every human ever born.

In this dream, I saw a big square and on top of the big square was a little square, which was like a head that had eyes and a brain. It looked like a big box man with no arms and no legs, just a stomach and a head. What I saw was consistent with the teachings and drawings I had seen through the years of my sobriety. In this dream there were five boxes going across the chest area of the larger box. They were negative emotional file boxes of sorts, which had negative emotions written under them. Under each one a word was written: hurt, rejection, anger, resentment and unforgiveness. Then on the lower or stomach area of the larger box were five positive emotional file boxes, labeled: love, joy, peace, happiness and self-control. When I was looking at it,

I saw thoughts in word sentences coming into the brain of the square box head and the brain was processing each thought. Everything we've heard or seen and everything ever done to us is processed and dropped down into a positive emotion or a negative emotion. In the center of all the boxes was a big void, a circle in the belly button area that I call the "Big Hole" of incompleteness which is in every human ever born. Sometimes I call it the "Big Black Hole of Loneliness" or the empty void. Over the last couple of years I have really sought out the meaning of this all. It did line up with drawings I had seen and teachings I had received in the past, but, I felt it was something deeper and more complex than I had ever imagined.

I will now attempt to explain why most of us are dealing with life controlling issues such as addiction, anger, overeating, gambling, pornography, depression, control, unforgiveness, rejection, resentment, bitterness, being judgmental, and so on. We try to fix these issues ourselves through so many diets, detox programs, medications, counseling and meetings, without much success. These efforts will not work long term and we will never be set completely free until we get an understanding of how we got the way we did in the first place. Then we can receive the instructions on how to get set free from it all.

So, put on your boots, we're about to go deep.

Like I said before, the soul is a combination of your mind, will and emotions. I also want to point out that we have positive emotional feelings and negative emotional feelings. This is how it works on the negative side, using myself as an example. The first negative incident I can remember as a kid was when I was seven years of age. My mom and dad split up and my dad moved out. As a seven year old I had negative feelings of rejection, hurt, anger, depression and confusion. I also had positive emotions, remembering the happiness I had at the time, because I always had my twin brother to play with me so I was never alone. You see, the real us is like a computer hard drive. From the day we are born we store every thought and action done to us as well as what we have done to others. Everything we see and hear, things other people say to us, and circumstances that happen to us, affect our emotions by giving us a positive or negative feeling.

Here is an example of the process: You're at work one day with a friend you've known for five years who works with you. Let's say you overhear your friend telling someone else how much he really does not like you. You feel stunned. Those words come into your ear gates which you process as positive or negative feelings/emotions. You process this, good or bad, and then store those feelings. The feelings of those five powerful words, (he really does not like you) may make you feel hurt, rejected, humiliated, inadequate, sad and so on. You store all of these emotions/feelings into separate boxes. The same thing happens with positive experiences. Most of us are aware that only so much can be stored on a computer. Your soul—the real you without God (your mind, will and emotions)—is a product of what you've stored in your emotional boxes from the day you were born until now. I'm convinced that most of us, from the time we are sixteen until twenty years of age, have our emotional boxes full of many undealt with negative emotions and misdirected positive emotions that are driven by the current world system of what the world considers love, joy, peace, happiness, and self-control. So, when we get to this point most of us are very open to life controlling behaviors because we cannot process or deal with new feelings or emotions. It is at this time that our soul turns to "first thought wrong," which is going with a false thought of how to deal with what has just happened.

What does this look like and what are you talking about? Again, I will use my story as an example. Experiences like divorce, sexual abuse, rape, rejection and so on can create many negative emotions. There are not many positive emotions because they can only be recalled after the bad starts to outweigh the good. This happens often when there is more negative than positive. We seem to forget or dismiss the feelings as positive. So it was in my story, and by the time I was twelve years of age, my soul was stuffed with many horribly negative emotions I had never dealt with, all piled on top of the empty void on the inside, this Big Black Hole of loneliness. I had already been introduced to alcohol and weed by the age of ten and although I did it as the thing to do with friends, I found out something really great about what it was doing for me at the time. When I smoked or drank I didn't feel the negative un-dealt with emotions anymore that I had constantly thought about (the sexual abuse, anger, rejection) and the Big Black Hole was being filled and I didn't feel empty and alone anymore. It was fun to do the mind altering substances and they filled my soul. I could only remember the good times, and although this was not the answer, it worked for me every time. I discovered that it also fixed "first thought wrong." I could not process my emotions because my soul's hard drive was full. I still had positive and negative emotions coming in all day. So now if some-one said something mean that hurt me or pissed me off, I could use drugs or alcohol and within seconds and stuff the negative emotions/feelings down and become numb to them. Over time I found out that when I came off the drugs/alcohol the empty black hole was there and all the voices of my undealt with emotions were screaming at me. At a very young age I became a person, like so many do, that searched for ways to always stay high and busy, so I was able to fill the void and stop the thoughts of all the painful things ever done to me or that I had ever done to anyone else.

It's really a wrong train of thought to think that using life controlling behaviors like drugs, sex and crime is because a person is just weak or a loser or a less than. But the truth is, using is our attempt to deal will our emotions and fill the black hole burning in inside of us. Don't be misled into thinking that it's only those who use drugs or alcohol who are affected. Many of you reading this book may be trying to un-derstand why others are addicted and afflicted and you have the same problems as they do, but you are able to deal with it without drugs or booze. You may not realize you use some other life controlling behavior such as food to deal with your emotions or porn, gambling, shopping, antidepressants, sports, or some other obsessive behavior. We all use something until we learn to take every thought captive and deal with it. Well, what other controlling behaviors do you mean? What does this look like? Let's look at some examples.

Food: A bad day at work. Someone disrespected you in front of everyone. You don't do drugs and alcohol because they are bad, so you come home and binge out by eating a ton of food. Then afterwards you feel bad and you throw it all up. Maybe you are going through some stressful situations in life. You are at home thinking about it, but you notice that all you do is open the refrigerator looking to eat or just crunch on something. This is called an emotional eater.

Medication: You get prescribed medication from a doctor in an attempt to deal with first thought wrong (which may be hurting yourself or others) from what has happened over the years. Depression pills for thirty years of undealt with emotions and you still have the big black void on the inside.

Sex: You're married, you even have a couple of kids, but the romance between husband and wife has gone cold. The wife still has some baby weight because she's a stay at home mom and she doesn't have time to get pretty. She's too tired to make advances towards you so you don't desire her any more. First thought wrong: "I'll just watch some porn online. I am not physically cheating, so it's not hurting anyone," you think. You feel pleasured and your empty hole is filled. This works for about a week and then you do it again and then it becomes a lifestyle because it works every time and never lets you down. It's fixing the first thought of, "I want to be loved through sex and I want to fill the hole of loneliness because my wife is not meeting my most major basic needs."

When we find "something" that will address shutting down the undealt feelings, satisfying first thought wrong and filling the hole of loneliness, we will stick with it as a way to maintain our life controlling behaviors. But things will get worse and worse causing us to add more life controlling behaviors to it. Why? Because we are continuing to add to the already existing undealt with emotions, and even without our life controlling behaviors we still have an empty void that leaves us unsatisfied whether we have a good life, a great job, a big home, wonderful marriage, life, family, etc. It is a never ending process that will end in death and destruction and misery for ourselves and our loved ones.

So let's recap. We are dealing with our soul which is our mind, will and emotions, which I am convinced is the real you. The soul works like this:

Mind: Someone says something to you; you take that thought and make a decision to put it in your emotional box, whether it's positive or negative; then you act on it (this is your will). Example: John comes up to Jerry and says you're a jerk in front of all Jerry's friends. Jerry takes that thought and sees it as disrespectful, hurtful, and Jerry feels angry and makes a decision out of his will to "monkey slap" John upside his head. You see, Jerry has to do something with the thought. But because Jerry, like most of us, has a full emotional box, he goes with first thought wrong, which is, "John hurt me and made me feel and look like a fool." So his will is to act out on the negative emotions that have just come into his soul because there is no room to process the thing that was said to him. Within our soul is also an empty void that we continue to try to fill through jobs, relationships, addictions, possessions, toys, sexual activities—anything we can find. Without a constant supply of these things and our life controlling behaviors, at the end of the day we are still empty and void with nothing to fully fill us unless it's a constant supply of medication, substances, drugs, alcohol, sex, etc. How do I know that? Let me assure you, if I could have kept my life together, had peace, and kept the empty hole filled by shooting dope, I would still be doing it. We will always stick with our life controlling behaviors and they will continue to get worse and worse, and we will continue to add more and more behaviors to our list. This is the human condition.

chapter seven

BAD SOIL

In the Bible Jesus explains that there are certain things that will steal the truth out of your hearts. He describes this in a story about seeds in good and bad soil. I believe the soil He is talking about is your soul. I have found that this empty void that we have is separate from our soul. We are like a seed that has to grow in good ground in order to produce fruit of real change.

You see, when you hear the truth and it does not make sense to you, it is lost in you or stolen out of your heart. Some hear the message of God and there is great excitement. They get jacked up but because there is no root, it is just an experience on bad soil (mind, will, and emotions); the seed never grows up. When affliction, addiction, or persecution comes many immediately fall away. Some hear the message of truth but the worries of life, emotions, pain, hurt, or the desire to get wealth choke out the Word and no fruit comes forth.

I am going to share some things in life that will keep the truth from growing in you and that deceptively temporarily fill that empty void.

We see people who go to church every week for many years and never see any real change in them. Why? It is because they do not have good ground for the seed of Christ to grow. Jesus reveals to us that what goes on in our lives directly relates to our souls (mind, will, and emotions) and there are things that prevent us from truly having good ground. Most of us have been sober many times. We've tried to follow the ways of God, we've begun a twelve step program or some other weight loss program, only to feel worse emotionally. We aren't realizing or understanding that our problem is not the life controlling behaviors, it is something deeper and more complex and if someone does not show us the way out we will never get escape. Don't worry, Jesus will never leave you hanging.

I have written a second section of this book that will go into more details to get you on 'good ground,' so daily you can produce a 'hundred, sixty and thirty-fold' fruit in your life. Notice that I put hundred fold first? I believe that by the time you're done with this book you will be able have one hundred-fold fruit in you. This means that your life will be as if you planted one seed and it produces a 100 pieces of fruit.

Let's look deeper into the one seed that is sown on good ground. Luke 8:15 says it like this, "But the seed in the good soil are the ones who have heard the word with an honest and good heart and hold fast and bear fruit with perseverance." The first thing that is key in this verse is coming to a point in life where you're honest about your need for change and your heart is good because you have taken the step to invite someone greater, someone outside of yourself, to come live in you, to fill your empty void. Without this happening the rest of this book will not work.

The only way to hold fast to the Word planted in you is by dealing with your emotions and not allowing the things mentioned in the three parables to steal your seeds, such as the cares of the world, temptations, pleasure of life, money, hurt pain, etc. The verse goes on to say something profound that most of us miss. It says, that one that bears thirty, sixty, one-hundredfold, with perseverance. That means that we must daily hold fast, deal with our emotions so that we are good ground, and over time will produce, "harvest exceeding his wildest dreams," (Mark 4:8 MSG).

It works the same way in our addiction. It took time to produce the bad fruit of addiction. I know I was committed to my life controlling behaviors and with perseverance and they produced bad fruits. Our whole lives have revolved around our emotions and our desire to escape from the bad ones. Breaking free requires at least the same amount of commitment that we had with our life controlling behaviors. As I was discovering the reason for my behaviors, my dream brought the Bible's words alive, making sense to me for the first time. Maybe I could help others see this same truth and keep them from the endless cycle I found myself in many times before. I had found my way off this drug induced ride and I really understood how to get off and stay off of it.

chapter eight

WHERE SON TRULY MEETS DADDY

In 2009 I became involved, and then began volunteering, with a faith-based recovery program in Titusville, Florida. This is where I truly learned about having a one-on-one, personal relationship with God. I sat under some of the best teachers and teachings to date concerning inner healing and soul healing, which were all based at Dunklin Memorial Camp. But more than anything, I learned about sharing my emotions with God through journaling and learned that when I was done talking, God would talk back to me.

Up until this point in my life, through God's help, I had broken free from all addictions. I had a godly wife but still felt unfulfilled. Over thirty years of undealt with emotions were festering inside me and because I was not properly dealing with my current emotions; I was heaping those on top of the pile. The next two years were life changing for both myself and my wife as we sat under these great teachers and teachings, applying what we'd learned to our own lives. The healing that happened to us was amazing!

Many of the things that I have shared as a speaker and have written in this book, have come from the knowledge I received in my two years involved in this faith-based recovery program and the rest is, as Paul says in the Bible, direct revelation from the Holy Spirit.

After my Jesus-given wife and I heard from the Lord that it was time to transition out of this program, I was offered an addiction counseling job in the secular field working in a group setting with clients that were charged with DUI's (Driving Under the Influence) and first time drug offenders. My boss at the time, who is still a close friend today, had been in the field for over forty years and seen fit to give me a chance despite my past. I was with the company for two years. While there I studied and took classes and was able to earn an Addiction Counseling Certificate. My wife and I started Bible College and it was there that we really started learning and actively using our gifts of the Spirit and it totally transformed our walk and drew us unto a deep relationship with the Lord.

I earned my Associates Degree in Theological Studies and when I began writing this book, my wife was two classes away from getting her Bachelor's Degree in Theology. After two years working with DUI's, I had a desire to get a better paying job in the healthcare field but I found with my past record it was impossible; I have thirteen felonies in my record. The only thing I could do was to go through the exemption process, proving that my life was extremely better and that I would be an asset to the health care field and not a liability.

While applying for a new job, a very well-known company hired me and was willing to wait for the exemption process to be completed. It was a very grueling process; I wanted to give up so many times. I went through month after month of being interviewed by a board of people in the health field, going over each and every felony I committed, reminding me of every detail of all the times I was arrested. Every time I stood before them to speak it seemed impossible, yet I kept persevering and pushing through it all. There were times I felt I was never going to have a decent job because of my record. At one point, even my wife and some of my family told me to give up, but something inside urged me to keep going. God was going to show off in a mighty way. This entire process took six months, but finally I was screened and my record cleared to work in the healthcare system as well as with the DCF (Department for Children and Families) to work with kids.

And the miracles didn't stop there—after four years of applying, I was accepted to be a Chaplin at the county jail near where we lived. God's awesomeness opened a door for me, with my thirteen felonies, to walk in and out of a jail without even being searched. It was, and still is, an outrageous miracle! The Chaplin told me he had men with DUI's from twenty years ago who did not pass and were unable to volunteer at the jail. Me, a Volunteer Chaplin? At a jail? Who would of thought? I was able now to teach faith-based addiction and inner healing classes.

You see, God can move the heart of anyone, when it is His will, despite your past. If He will do it for me, He will do it for you.

I was so glad! I felt on top of the world. This showed me how big God is and that nothing is impossible for Him and I was going to tell the whole world of what God had done in my life! He can open doors that no man can open.

After 8 months I was doing great at this new job, making really good money, but deep down inside I knew that I wanted to be back full time in faith-based recovery.

God started giving me visions of creating a self-sustaining, faith-based in-patient recovery facility. Everything was going great, and nearly a year into my new job, I was offered the position of director of a fairly new faith-based recovery program. My deepest longing was for the program to be self-sustaining through creating businesses and cultivating the land for food. The vision that the Lord gave me laid this plan out very clear. At first my wife said no to the job, but a couple of days later she said she felt the Lord was telling us to be open to it. This amazed me! Of course many people were blown away that I got this great job; what many considered a high profile job. People go to school for years and years just to get a shot at this company that I had been working for. I shared with a few friends that I was considering this offer as a director and they were all saying, "After everything you went through to get exempt where you're at, and now you're going to leave it?" Nobody could understand.

What they didn't understand is that I had been in both the secular and faith-based fields and I had not seen one person, out of many, truly get whole and free in every area of their life. 95% of those treated always went back to full blown addiction. I knew in my heart something was missing.

While I was working at this great job with this great company, I received three job offers to oversee and direct faith-based recovery programs. It was also at this time I had the dream about the box man with the positive and negative emotions, that I told you about a couple of chapters back, which gave me a deeper revelation on why people stayed addicted.

My wife and I stepped out in faith, left it all, and gave it a shot. Many thought it was the wrong move, but this is what you must do to follow your dreams. Leave it all!

chapter nine

LESSONS AND VISION

We sent our vision to those who offered the position and decided we would fast and pray to get an answer from the Lord. After the end of the appointed fast we felt the peace of God and that's when we decided to leave job, home and security for the Kingdom. It was exciting and wonderful and after the first year I learned many valuable lessons that would carry me the rest of my life. The first thing was, although God gave me a vision of what a Kingdom program looks like for me, it did not mean that vision was the same for others.

Lesson 1: If you're coming into someone else's leadership and vision, find out what their vision is and ask often about it before you enter in agreement. If you're not willing to follow all of their vision, don't do it.

Lesson 2: I learned about my gifting. I love inner/soul healing in a group setting, but more than that I love doing it one-on-one. During this time, while being a director at this recovery program, I found out that I was not gifted in disciplining men concerning rules and attitudes.

A wise man, Dr. Bob, shared this statement with me. He said, "You have to ask yourself, does your temperament match your gifting or what you're actively serving in and if it does not, it probably is not your calling."

I was working in a one year in-patient program setting, housing up to six men. Everything was going great until someone in the house shared with me what was going on behind closed doors. At this time I started to deal with the men in a more correctional type of way and I despised it. After a while I lost my love and desire for what I was doing, but that was okay. I found out God did not gift me with the temperament to correct and discipline. He called me to mentor, disciple, and walk people through soul healing, helping them start and stay in a daily one-on-one relationship with The Void Filler.

What Dr. Bob told me was the deciding factor of stepping away from this last faith-based recovery setting. My dream and my goal through this book is to open a counseling center with short term housing for men and women and to walk them through their healing in a safe place, as well as creating businesses and connections, giving people like you and me a new start. A large portion of the money made from this book will be used towards making this dream come true. It has been the dream of so many to create a community of people that want to stay set free. We can do this together—one person a time.

chapter ten

TRUE FREEDOM IS TIME WITH YOUR MAKER

If I could take all the information I wrote in this book and wrap everything up into one chapter, it would be this one. Time with your Maker is the biggest key to healing and staying healthy, whole, mature, and free in all areas of life.

You and I meet with something every day to get our day going. It is either with undealt emotions from the past and fighting for another inch to drive wider the empty void on the inside of your soul, or you will read this very carefully and learn how to meet with the God that made you and loves you very much. Maybe you don't even believe in God and that's okay; He believes in you. He made you and has not given up on you.

In the book of John it says God the Father and the Lord Jesus will come to live inside of us and leave the Holy Spirit with us to teach, comfort, convict us, and much more. It is very deep, and hard to grasp it all, so I will try my best to share with you what I believe has been the number one key to my staying sober, happy, and prosperous in all things pertaining to life and godliness. This does not mean that everything will always be perfect, but that we can learn to process our thoughts, feelings and emotions in a one-on-one relationship with our Creator instead of meeting one-on-one with our life controlling behaviors like addiction, food, sex, control, anger, depression, guilt, and a list of behaviors that can go on and on.

What To Do

First things first. You must be open to invite Jesus to fill your empty void and come into your life by allowing the Holy Spirit to lead and guide you through a daily one-on-one relationship with the Father. This is the only way this will work for you. If you have not done this, take some time to do so. There are many different ways to do this. I say, make it your own and pray:

God, a lot of this doesn't make sense to me and I may not even believe there is a God, but I have been using my undealt with emotions and my life controlling behaviors to try to fill this empty void in my life and it is not working. Will You and Jesus come live inside of me and fill this void? Thank you for coming to live inside of me. Teach me Your ways and show me what is important to You. Forgive me for all of my sins and all those I have sinned against. Help me to see myself the way You see me and to love myself the way You love me. Thank you.

Anything along those lines will work. God is not into to some five-word prayer that is perfect. He is into a pure heart that is truly calling out for help, so just make it your own.

What I Personally Do

When I wake up each morning I go to my quiet spot that I have just for God and me to meet. I get up earlier than my wife, most of the time, and like it this way, because I really need alone time with no noise in order to truly get what I need out of my time with the Lord. It was no different than when I was shooting drugs to deal with my emotions and to get my day started. I was committed to it and could do nothing at all in life until I got those drugs into my veins. If I didn't I could not function, move, or even get out of bed.

When we let go of our life controlling behaviors and turn to God to fulfill these needs, we have to have the same mindset—that if I don't get what I need from meeting with my Creator that I will go back to what was working for me for the last ten, twenty, thirty, forty years. It worked every time and we will continue to go back if we don't learn to meet with the only True One who can fill the void. Jesus died to restore the empty void that was created when Adam did the one thing God told him not to do—he ate from the tree of good and evil.

The Lord told Adam if he ate of the tree he would die. This death was what caused the empty void that's in every human ever born. This was what we lost, our rightful fulfillment and connection with God himself. Only inviting Him back in can restore this empty void. It's not a onetime thing it is a daily thing. Just like our life controlling behaviors.

I get to my quiet spot, get out my journal, and write a letter to God about how I felt about yesterday. I truly share my heart and the good things that I'm thankful for. For an example, read the Psalms. David, the only man God called a man after His own heart, praises God with thanksgiving, tapping in to this one thing that arrested God's heart enough to say, "Now this is a man after my own heart." I always write what I'm thankful for first and take some time to tell God how much I love and appreciate my many blessings like, coffee, cold water, a home, a wonderful wife, and so on. Being thankful will help you to see that not much in life is really worthy of storing permanently into your emotions.

Most importantly, I search my heart to see if there were any negative undealt with emotions that crossed my soul yesterday. Did I treat anyone in an unworthy manner? Did anyone treat me in a way that made me feel less than, angry, hurt, etc.? A good thing to do is ask the Holy Spirit to reveal to you if there is anything on the inside that you did not process or deal with. If you did not take the thought captive and deal with it, then you stored it in one of your negative emotional boxes on the inside, and when they get filled you and I only know one way to deal with them and that is through our life controlling behaviors.

The question is how do we take a negative thought captive before it becomes a feeling or an emotion? So we've taken time to thank God for all the good things that happened yesterday, and how He has blessed us. Now it's time to get some things off your chest that were put into your soul, affecting you in a negative manner.

Below is an example of a negative emotion and how to take the thought captive and deal with it positively in a letter to God. Once your relationship and knowledge grows, you will see that you can talk to Father God, Jesus, and The Holy Spirit all in the same letter, but for now we will keep it with Our Father, I like to call him Papa Bear, Papa Dog, Daddy, Father, and Abba.

Letter To Our Daddy (written May 11, 2015)

"Good morning, Papa Bear. Thank You for this fine Monday morning. Thank You for waking me up. Been having some weird dreams lately, please reveal anything you are trying to say to me. Thank You for allowing Sandra and I to go to the beach yesterday. It was a beautiful day. Grateful that we had the money to go. Thank You for always providing for all our needs and for many of our wants. You are truly a good Daddy. Yesterday was Mother's day, I felt badly for Sandra. Lord how we have longed for a son that you have promised for almost eight long years! Although it has not happened yet, I still have not given up hope. I think Sandra may have given up hope, but I know that You cannot lie and way too many people who do not even know us have prayed over us concerning this. Sandra and I got into it a little, over me wanting to get a milkshake and chicken fries. She has been very moody lately since she has been on this diet. I have thought about maybe life would be easier on my own. I know these are wrong thoughts and ask you to restore our marriage into what you desire it to be. Reveal to me where I can make things better. I have really been trying, by buying some gifts and being sweet, but I still say comments that I know hurt her. Daddy, help me and forgive me for being this way. Help me to be a kind and loving husband that builds her up with my words, and help me to support and honor her diet. Reveal to me if I have said things that hurt her, and open a door for me to go and ask her forgiveness. She said when I eat bad stuff it's like putting crack in front of her. I don't want to make her feel like that. We did not talk the whole way home after the beach. This is the first time this has ever happened in our eight years of marriage. Lord, we also have not been to church in over a month due to us both feeling we need to pull back and rest and re-evaluate where you have called us and why we were going. We both felt like we were going to church out of obligation and neither of us were getting anything out of the messages. I can tell a difference in both of our attitudes. Lord, I miss truly hearing Your word and experiencing Your presence. It seems like the more we don't go the easier it is not to go. Lead us to where You want us to go and give us the courage to go. Lead us to Your will and put a deep desire in Sandra and my heart to do it. Bless our new Bible study we are starting this Wednesday. Lord, yesterday after our time at the beach I truly wondered, "What am I doing with my life?" Thank You for allowing me to write in our book *Addicted No More*. Daddy, I leave yesterday in the past and lay it at Your feet. Thank You for allowing Sandra to come to me and rebuild the bridge by asking me to forgive her for being so moody. Lord, help us both to look ahead to what we know is coming from You. Very excited about our California trip that is happening in three weeks. Clean Sandra and I both from any undealt with emotions and bless us today in Jesus' name. Lord, bless my time with Danny T. as we work at the dealership with Kevin, Chris, and Mike. Use me to be Your shining light on this earth and allow me to draw others closer to You. Open doors for me to talk to others about You and to cast out demons and heal the sick and to set the captives free. Today is a new week for Sandra and me, allow it to be great and glorious in You my Father, Friend, and Daddy.

Next Step

This is a real letter that is true of what happened May 11, 2015. I was able to get real and share my heart with God about all the feelings and emotions that happened that day. I went to bed with these feelings and woke up with them. It is important to ask the Lord to reveal any undealt with emotions so they can be cleared up daily.

When you do this, these thoughts and emotions will be fresh on your mind when you wake up so, they will be easy to write and deal with. Now that you have done this you have cleaned your soul so that you have good ground. This next thing you do is the most important. Up until this day most of us have found our love, joy, peace, and happiness from what the world says will bring you these things, which is your job, wife, sex, money, family, children, house, car, friends, hobbies, food and so on. But most of you reading this have had all of these things in abundance and it still was not enough to fill the void or complete your happiness.

Today and from this day forward you have to get your love, joy peace, and happiness from hearing what your Father says to you about yesterday and today. So when I'm done sharing my heart I then ask my Daddy the question: "WHAT WOULD YOU LIKE TO SAY TO ME MY GOD AND FRIEND?" If you have invited Him to live in you then you can hear from Him at any time you choose. Imagine what a good Daddy would say to His son or daughter. He would say that He loves you and remembers none of your sins. He looks at you as if you had never committed a sin and never will commit another. Many times as God speaks to you it is an inner voice inside that sounds just like your voice, because you are made in His likeness and in His image. Let's complete this. I asked our Daddy the question and recorded what He said to me about my day on May 11, 2015.

What Would You Like To Say To Me My God and Friend?

"Hello, my beloved son and good morning to you. Thank you, Jason for taking time to meet with me and put down how I speak to you in our book *Addicted No More*. Jason, I know you felt badly for Sandra about you both not having a child yet. I want you to know that I have a plan for you both and that I'm sorry that you have not had a child yet. I'm not being mean my son, but want you to know that my plans don't always make sense at the time and can seem like a punishment, but don't believe the enemy's lies. If I promised it I will bring it to pass in my time. Thanks, my son, for not giving up hope and always trusting in me.

Jason, thank you for considering Sandra's feelings and not getting the fast food. It did make you mad and have thoughts of being alone; that truly was selfishness. Son, you know I always forgive you and love to see you work through things. Be kind towards your wife and my beloved daughter. She is really trying hard to be healthier which is a good thing my son. Jason, you have a mission and a purpose and a plan and until you get there you will often have questioning thoughts about what you are doing with your life. This is what drives you to keep seeking me. Idle time causes this. When you are feeling this way think of productive things you can do that will draw us closer. Jason, I'm also excited about the California trip that is coming up in three weeks. It will be life changing for both Sandra and you. I will connect you with those that will be part of your life-giving destiny for the world. You will be a world changer and help millions of those addicted and afflicted. Jason, more than any of that, you will lead others to have a one-on-one, personal two-way relationship between my children and me. Talk about being excited, son! I'm super stoked about this and can't wait. We are going to do great things together. Well, son, I know you have to get to work. Go forth and be a shining light to those I put in front of you. I will open doors for you to heal others and to be a blessing. Just offer to do it, and don't even think about it. I have called you to it, so heal the sick and set the captives free, my son. Jason, love your wife and continue to go the extra mile to show forth this love. I know Sandra and you have not been to church in over a month and you're feeling the effects of it. So try something new. Son, I'm good with you both for I know your hearts are towards me. I love you so much, son, and thanks for putting down what I say to you.

All those who are reading this I want you to know I love you so very much and I'm not mad at you, but madly in love with you. I have longed for this day since the day you were born. I want to spend time with you every day and hear your heart. I want to hear all the good things and bad things and sad things. I want you to share your dreams with Me and your disappointments. Most of all I want to talk back to you, so please give Me a chance. The devil will lie to you many times and say this is not God; it is you making it up. Don't listen to the lie. I live in you and have made My home in you and am always ready to talk to you. I'm so very proud of you for opening yourself up to let Me to come fill your void. I invite you to cast all your cares on Me for I care for you. I love you and will be looking forward to our first letter together. See you then!

Your Daddy

- Love you, J-Dog, and talk to you soon. Today is going to be awesome. I have set blessings before you my son, so walk in them."

Let me assure you when your Father talks to you like this every day you will be truly fulfilled and will never go back to anything less!

Another Example of taking each thought captive:

Yesterday your coworker John called you lazy. You go home feeling pissed, upset, worthless, and so on. When you sit down the next day and share with the Lord how you feel, you say, "Lord, John called me lazy. It hurt me and pissed me off. Was I acting in a way that would cause him to say this? I don't want to store these thoughts and feelings in to my emotions, Lord, so I lay them at your feet and ask you to open a door for me to talk to John about how I feel and if John is struggling with something, give me wisdom to see this so that I may pray for him. He may be hurting and said this out of his pain. Thank you, Lord, for taking this negative feeling from me. Fill me with Your peace and let me see myself as You see me and to see and love John the way You do."

We must do this for each and every negative thought that comes into our soul daily. If we don't, we will build up negativity and will not be able to process our thoughts because our undealt with emotions will turn into other undealt with emotions. Our emotional boxes will fill back up until we cannot process what is in them and then we will automatically return to first thought wrong.

Take Time to Know God

After our time talking to Daddy and Him talking to us, I always take time to read His Word. It is what He left to us to reveal who He is and how He does things and how we are to do things. Please caution yourself not to get caught up in following a religion or a man for your knowledge of God. If you want to know Him, read His Word daily (Bible). Jesus said if you want to see the Father look at Him. He said He was the exact representation of the Father. A good place to start is in the books of John, Psalms, and Proverbs. The way your faith is built is by Romans 10:9: "Faith comes by hearing, and hearing by the Word of God." (Romans 10:17 NKJV). I like to read out loud sometimes. Take time to put a worship song on and allow His presence to overtake you. I do not do the song thing a lot, but my wife loves it. Don't forget most of you reading this have been feeding on the world's TV, music, hobbies and so on for ten, twenty, thirty, forty, fifty, and even sixty years. If you truly want a changed life you have to have a renewed mind in order to be truly transformed. A look at Romans 12:1-2 will give you a better understanding of this.

Love, Joy, Peace and Happiness

Now that we have dealt with the negative, we must get our love, joy, peace, and happiness by the things our Daddy God told us when we ask Him what He wanted to say. Daddy God is always going to build you up and tell you delightful things and in the same process let you know when you need to tighten up. The key is that when you walk out of your alone time to face His purpose for your life each day, that you are starting each day with good ground that is open to receive a 30-, 60-, 100-fold harvest.

You have dealt with your soul (mind, will, emotions) and you have heard from your Daddy. We don't have to look to what the world looks to for happiness to fill the void. We have just met with The Void Filler. We don't have to look to our job, wife, husband, kids, home, money, friends, life or controlling behaviors, for we have been filled by God speaking to us about us. This is what we must do daily to deal with to-day's emotions. Later in Part 2, we will go back and sort through your past emotions.

To date I have never met a person who met with God in the morn-ing and later that day he smoked crack. So keep your head high there is hope for you. The key is being more committed to your relationship with God than you are to your addictions/life controlling behaviors.

chapter eleven

GETTING HIGH ON THE HOLY SPIRIT

This Chapter is not for everyone, but this as an important chapter for those of us who have been in the drug and alcohol world or anything that alters your state of mind into a euphoric feeling.

Over the years of following the Lord and allowing the Holy Spirit to take residence in me through the infilling of His power, I have found that every mind altering substance was in fact a counterfeit to the infilling power of the Holy Spirit. Every high I personally have ever felt from mind altering substances has been overpowered by the high the Holy Spirit has given me. The high from Holy Spirit will jack you up better than shooting dope of any kind in your veins.

Those who have not dealt with drugs, but have dealt with food addiction, sex addiction, gambling, and so on—all of these give us a euphoric feeling when we do them and also attempts to fill the empty void on the inside. I will confess to everyone reading this that if you don't find a high better than the high caused by your life controlling behaviors you will return to them over time, every time.

I have personally worked with many that had one, two, three years sober in a Christian community in-patient recovery program, and I have seen many, after a week of being released, go right back to full addiction. Over the years I have searched the factors of why this happens and this is what the Lord revealed to me.

While in recovery they never fully gave one-hundred percent Lordship to Christ. How one knows this, is through fruit. We become new creations in Christ Jesus. If the Holy Spirit is living in you and you are good ground and have dealt with your life of undealt with emotions, then you, as a person, should change in a mighty way. This does not mean you are perfect, but that you are bearing fruit of the Holy Spirit. This personally did not happen for me until I receive the infilling or as some call it, the baptism of the Holy Spirit. Jesus told the disciples He would baptize them with the Holy Spirit and Fire. A lot of people get a weird feeling about this subject, but those of us coming from deep addiction were willing to get very weird in our addiction.

We know that after Jesus was crucified the disciples were on the run and in hiding, but after the day the Holy Spirit came to them in Spirit and Fire they became bold and high on the Spirit to the point of dying for this infilling experience. Many of us are on our way to death with our life controlling behaviors. If something doesn't change in order to do this justice, we must turn to the Word of God to see what it says about this, then you can make a personal decision as to what is truth. I'm convinced that without this truth none of this book matters or will have any real lasting effect on your life for the long haul. I have worked with many that follow the truths in this book, but without the availability to get high on the Most High we will return to the counterfeit high of this world system. I know it sounds crazy, but those of us coming from deep substance addiction can relate.

Don't misunderstand me; I am not trying to use Holy Spirit to get my buzz or my feel good. I assure you, when the Holy Spirit jacks you up on a high that wrecks you and it is ten times better than any dope high, you will be much less likely to ever go for a fake high that leaves you wanting and miserable every time you come down. Yes, this seems a bit gangster and most likely a different approach to getting high. There are few ways I personally have identified that allow me to access the power of the Holy Spirit in such a way that it alters my mind and body.

- When the Lord opens a door for me to use my gifting.
- Music involved in worship. (for me this is 1.1.SIX Crew, Christian Rap)
- Giving thanks to God about His goodness invokes this high.
- Daily spending alone time with Him each morning through prayer, journaling, and Bible reading I feel His power.
- Encouraging others in the Lord when they are going through tough times.
- Listening to another share the Word that is Holy Spirit inspired.
- Reading books that are Holy Spirit inspired.

When I do these things many times I feel the power of the Holy Spirit come over me and at times I feel chills and goose bumps, other times it's like electricity coming in and out of my body, other times His power and greatness breaks me into weeping and crying. There are times where the Holy Spirit living inside of me will jump like bouncing a ball on the ground in my stomach and my whole insides shake.

I know this is wild and many of you have never heard of this. With the infilling of the Holy Spirit I also received a prayer language. I don't know all the facts on it, but if you read the book of Acts it will explain it more.

This I do know, that in order for us to be able to stop getting high we have to experience something better than the high that we have experienced. This is through the infilling of the Holy Spirit. If you want this same experience, I'm convinced that you can receive it where you are right now, all alone by yourself. The Bible has a passage that reads like this: "If you, being evil know how to give good gifts to your children, how much more will *your* heavenly Father give the Holy Spirit to those who ask Him!" (Luke 11:13 NKJV)

You and I cannot make it without supernatural power. If you need this—and you do—trust me, I'm convinced that you can ask our Father for it right this minute and He will infill you with the power of the Holy Spirit.

Sample Prayer:

"Father, I realize I need something greater than myself to live a life pleasing to you and to my family. I need you to lead me and guide me into Your ways. Will you please infill me right now with the power of the Holy Spirit? Holy Spirit, come and fill me now with your power that I may live a life fulfilling to my Father. Jesus, live Your life through me and allow the promise of Holy Spirit to infill me, like it did You and your disciples. I love you, Father, and I thank and love you, Jesus, for dying for me and leaving the Holy Spirt to infill me, teach, lead and guide me. Thank you, Holy Spirit, for infilling me and living in me. Bless me with all the gifts that come with the infilling of You, Holy Spirit. I love you and thank you for this new life. In Jesus Name, Amen."

Brother and Sister, I assure that when you do this you better watch out! Without a doubt, you will get straight high and jacked up on what I like to call, "That Holy Ghost Juice," for sure! Get you some of that good, good! (My bad, some of my gangster coming out.)

WARNING:

Being filled with the Holy Spirit is a powerful gift that you have to steward. The Holy Spirit's infilling power cannot dwell in a soul of undealt with emotions or a soul on bad ground. You have to stay current in your daily relationship with Him. The quickest way to see His power leave is through the purposeful practice of sin, unforgiveness, resentment or undealt with anger. Take time to get into the Bible and look for some books that will explain some of what I'm sharing with you in a deeper context if you need more answers. If this whole Holy Spirit thing is weird to you, put in on the shelf and ask God to reveal the truth to you about this.

chapter twelve

TALKING NORTH AND WALKING SOUTH

Over all these years of recovery I have noticed one major thing that is most common in relapse—people having hidden areas they have not worked on or let go. Either we are 100 percent, to the best of our ability, doing the right thing in all areas, or we are not. Most of us in addiction have no middle ground. You cannot be sober and still lie, cheat, and hate. I call it 'sobriety religion.' Yes, this is just like church religion. You can talk all the church you want, but if your lips do not line up with your hips it is meaningless.

Jesus himself had a lot to say about this and those he spoke to were the leaders of what we would call churches of that time. He told many of those leaders that they were hypocrites and sons of the devil. He also said that there would be many in that day who would say to Him, "But Lord, we cast out demons, healed the sick and did many mighty miracles in your name. Yet He will say to them, 'Depart from me you who practices lawlessness. I never knew you!'" We have many people in the name of Jesus doing the things of God and getting results, yet in their private lives they practiced lawlessness. (Luke 7:22-23)

The most important part of our recovery is honesty and integrity in every area of our lives. This is the only way it will work! Truthfully, as of this day, I have not witnessed many fully walk this out in all areas of their lives. The reality is most having no idea what honesty and integrity means and how to identify if we are practicing lawlessness. What each of us must grasp is that if we have been addicted for one, five, ten, twenty, thirty, forty years, more than likely we have picked up many things that we do and say that are not in line with what God has for us.

As an example: We can't get sober and then grow and sell cannabis illegally and say it's okay because it's natural and God made it. Also, it is not okay to get sober from one thing and then decide it's perfectly fine to have a few beers, pills, cannabis and so on. We say, "As long as I'm not shooting heroin, I'm good." I know this to be true because I've done it. If we want God's best for us we have to be sober in all areas.

If you want to know the things important to God you have to get to know what He likes and what He dislikes and allow that to be your measuring stick. The Holy Spirit living in you is the One who will truly reveal these things to you. Listen to Him if you want true freedom in every area of your life—this is the, "narrow road that leads to life." It's not about rules and religion it's about your relationship being so great with God that you don't do the things the world does; this is what sets you apart from the world. (Matthew 7:14)

In the beginning of my recovery I chose the things I wanted to do. I still smoked, drank, lusted for other women, lied, and broke the law by going out having a few drinks while taking my pain meds and then driving. I even hit someone during a black out from pain meds and alcohol, all the while attending church, reading my Bible daily and praying. I woke up and my car was crashed and I had no idea what had happened.

I received a letter few months later saying I was involved in a hit and run and had six charges against me. I denied it at the time because I couldn't remember what had happen. I went to court to plead not guilty and the person who said I had hit them did not show, so the charges were dropped. After reading the report a few days later on what had happened, it all came back to me and I remembered the hit and run.

This was because I was still medicated on pain pills and alcohol and was not in my right mind. I had never crossed from religion into relationship until I was fully sober—off all meds that altered my mind.

When I did finally get off the meds and alcohol I started to relate and hear God like I had never experienced. The Lord started speaking to me about things I had never heard a preacher or church talk about or live out. One day I was driving and the Lord spoke to my heart, like you hear a voice out loud, about going over the speed limit.

He said, "Jason, most sins people commit are one time things that are over with very quickly. When you are driving over the speed limit you are in constant rebellion to the authority. You know if you see a cop you will slow down because you are doing wrong and you know the consequences of getting a ticket. Why is it okay for you to speed but not okay for others to smoke a joint or tell a lie or cheat on their taxes or wife?"

This hit my heart like a ton of bricks. I had met pastors and other leaders that were willing to do things like this, but why was God talking to me about things like this? The Lord then said to me, "You are set apart and if you want to help others in addiction you will have to live a life set apart."

I can tell you one thing about those in addiction that is an incredible quality—it is our sense to read people very well. If we see someone breaking a rule or a law or showing favoritism towards others, we form a judgement and never receive from that person again. I have known many people who went through recovery programs and got nothing out of it because they saw the one who was supposed to be an example, not living it out in their own lives. This is what Brother Rick calls, "shucking and jiving."

We are all at different places in our recovery and relationship with God. We, as recovering people, cannot allow what others do or don't do to highjack our recovery or relationship with God. One of the greatest influences in my life was a person called Brother Rick A. He walked the walk and talked the talk. Although he did not know it, he instilled in me some of the greatest lessons, which I attribute to my complete recovery.

I will call it what he often called it. He always said that you cannot 'walk north and talk south.' When you are fully committed to your recovery and your relationship with God your hips will line up with your lips. I was never able to truly hear what the Holy Spirit was saying to me about my recovery until I obeyed what He was revealing to me about my walk and talk, which I still have to work on daily.

As a counselor, I'm very mindful about obeying the rules and the laws of the land to the best of my ability. We are representing the Kingdom of God. If I do what everyone else is doing, such as stealing cable and internet, then I have violated what God has said to me personally. What He says to me about certain things, He may not say to you. The key is getting to a place where you can hear Him talking to you about your growth not everyone else's.

There is no in middle ground with people in addiction. Either we are all in, in all areas of our lives, or we are on a slow or fast road back to deep dark addiction. If you truly want to be set free and filled with the Holy Spirit, to the point where you can hear Him talk to you daily about the person He has called you to be, then you must stop shucking and jiving.

When we talk north and walk south, many times we create a false god in our likeness. The Bible calls it an idol. This happens often when people get out of jails, prisons, counseling and programs. They have been smoke free for six months and know smoking is bad for them and know God wants them to have their best health. After time they try a smoke. It is nasty and they feel bad and may ask God to forgive them. Smoking is not a heaven or hell issue, just as many of these other things that I'm talking about. But then they smoke again, and after time, harden their hearts to what the Holy Spirit has said to them. Before long they are no longer convicted about it. Once that happens many get into lust, etc., and before you know it, are back into full-blown addiction. I know these examples because I've done them all.

This is not about the law or obeying a bunch of rules or we won't make it to heaven. When you have a true relationship with the Lord we value what He wants for us, so we obey what He says out of honor, not because we have to do it. This does not mean we are going to get it right every time. Brother Rick used to say that sometimes it's one step forward and two steps back. The key is that we keep moving.

I wanted to end this book with the best advice I feel will keep you on the straight and narrow. I am speaking to both you and me when I say this—that we must have the highest integrity and truthfulness in all areas of our lives. I do not believe one can truly stay sober if they do not live in a way that sets them apart from others. I personally believe that when you're not living to the best of your ability in all areas that it blocks you from fully hearing what God wants to say to you daily.

Throughout our lives of addiction most of us have lost the trust of others so the truest sign that we have changed is the urgency to clean up the messes we've made and live in such a way that others would say that something has changed in us. You can do this and there is hope for you. Never give up!

chapter thirteen

2017 WHAT'S REALLY HAPPENING?

During this whole process, my wife Sandra was constantly praying for me and God's will for our lives. She was having recurring dreams of California, it was a bit odd because we never discussed it or even planned to visit the state. Her dreams consisted of us walking through the Pacific Coast, all the way to the north of California. But the most significant dream was when we were both walking towards a mountain covered with snow and we ended up in a community of believers where she saw the Kingdom of Heaven. She expressed a lot of dreams of California, but really, I never paid attention to it.

In the meantime, we left the faith-based recovery program and decided to take a break from recovery counseling. To be honest, we dropped anything that had to do with ministry, church, or Bible college and just wanted to take a sabbatical from everything. In this season of resting is where we both gained more growth than ever before and we both realized we both were operating out of performance.

Sandra saw that there was a writer's workshop in an amazing church in Northern California named Bethel Church. She saw this as a perfect opportunity to get to California and for me to connect with like-minded people concerning this book. And just like that, we took the trip to California. We landed in Los Angeles, and drove the Pacific Coast to Northern California; it was-of course, Epic. We also decided that we would really look for signs and confirmations from the Lord to see if He was calling us to move to there.

We made it to Redding, CA just in time for the writer's conference. It was a four-day conference. It was great; the speakers and worship were off the chain. By the third day I personally did not have any desires where I felt I wanted to move, or any special confirmations from the Lord to move. However, we noticed that in this land there was a great need to set many free from addiction.

The last day of the conference I remembered that Kris V., one of the Senior Pastors of this church, spoke. I had seen Kris preach once or twice. I personally thought he was cocky. Now that I have processed what I was feeling with him, I am cocky and identified with this. He was just a "keeping it real" kind of guy, which I like.

We headed back to Florida. We both agreed that neither one of us felt any confirmations from the Lord to move to Redding, CA while we were there. Boy, was I happy about this, because I never wanted to move out of Florida. I love it there and was feeling like God was on my side about this. Now Sandra, on the other hand, started feeling like Redding, CA was her home, and starting feeling like she was "homesick." She could not get it out of her head so we could move on from these dreams.

My wife and I, since we've been married, had moved nine times, been part of several recovery programs, attended Bible College for several years, sold everything, gave things away, tried to find our way, but most importantly, tried to discover God's will in our lives. We both were still healing and recovering emotionally from our time in ministry. For both us, the feeling of "being settled" felt like a relief, and if God told us to move again, it would be a big step of faith to move again.

A few weeks later, after being back from Redding, I started to wonder if we missed something from the Lord about moving to California. In my daily journal time, I asked Him, "Lord did we miss your calling us to Redding?" The Lord said to me, "You're not even open to if I was calling you to Redding." In my journal, in big letters in a cocky-type manner, I said, "Lord I Am Open to It."

I finished my quiet time and went to work. This day I was detailing cars at a used car dealership. Many of these cars are full of trash because they are bought at auction. The first car I started to work on had to be cleaned out so I started. On the back side of the driver's door seat there was a place you could put things in. In this little cubby hole I found a full-size college text book. I turned it over and guess what? The front cover was the picture of the Sundial Bridge in Redding, CA.

We walked on the Sundial Bridge the last day we were in Redding. I still have the book. After finding this the Lord had my attention. There was no way that I could tell the Lord I was open to Him revealing to me if He called us to move, and then a few hours later find a book in Florida with a picture of a bridge in Redding that we had walked on.

This was a little wild but I had been known to do wild things for His calling. I told The Lord that maybe I had missed something. I also said a book is not enough to have us sell two businesses, leave a 21-year-old daughter, dad, twin brother, older brother, sister, grandmother, aunts, uncles, and mom in North Carolina. I said, "Lord you have given Sandra many dreams about California. I have never had any dreams about California. If you will give me a dream about Redding and our call to move there I would be willing to really consider it. He said He would reveal to me if He wanted us to move.

So, I started asking the Lord to give me a California dream. About two weeks later He gave me two very wild dreams. Here is what they were:

DREAM # 1

In the dream, I was with students from Bethel School of Supernatural Ministry (BSSM) in Redding, CA. We were on a road that had a sharp turn. There was a ditch along that sharp turn. When the students and I walked down into the ditch it led us to a very old bridge. When we got under the bridge it transported us into a heaven-like portal. We were jumping in and out of it and then suddenly I was sitting in Bill J.'s office, the Senior Pastor of Bethel Church in Redding, CA.

While sitting with Bill in my dream, he was talking to me but I could not make out what he was saying. While he was talking to me, a lady came into the office and started prophesying over him, then suddenly, she turned into words and the words became a small whirlwind, like a small tornado of words that entered his body and became one with him. She was gone and I woke up. This dream startled me because of how real it was and the fact that I had never had any dreams of this sort ever in my life. After this the Lord really had my attention. I did not know what the dream meant and still don't, but I am sure the Lord will show me one day.

I shared with the Lord that He truly had my attention, but said to Him that Gideon asked for more than one sign with the fleece. I told Him if He would give me one more dream that I would be fully convinced and leave it all and move to Redding. He said He would do it.

DREAM # 2

A couple of weeks went by and I had another dream. This time I was with Kris V. who is the co-founder of the BSSM school. I was on a large piece of property which belonged to him. Kris walked with me to the left corner of his property and there stood a young apricot tree with two small clusters of apricots on it. I said to Kris, "Your apricot tree looks identical to the one I have at my home," (although I had no land or apricot tree) and he said, "Yes, I have been working on an apricot Dijon salad dressing. Kris said, "Come up to the house and we will try it." So we went up to his home and he had a bowl of fresh greens cut in 2-inch by 2-inch squares with the rib of the green in the middle of the square. There was nothing else in the salad, just the greens, and he put on the dressing. We ate it and it was off the chain. We then both walked out of his house to the property, the gates opened, and some Bethel members started coming in and walking all over his property. Then I woke up.

These two dreams were so realistic that every time I think of them I recall them perfectly. They were what I call mushroom acid-type visual-dreams. If you have ever done these drugs, then you know what I'm talking about. After twenty years, I can still remember some mushroom and acid trips. Very weird God dreams that I have not figured out, but know the Lord will bring them to pass. I now understand that these types of dreams are prophetic dreams send from Heaven.

The Lord told me, "I am sending you to Redding to break the back of addiction and connect with the ones I've revealed to you." He also revealed to me that meaning of the apricot tree, which I don't have the permission to release at this moment, but can tell you that is a "blueprint" from heaven, in others words, gave me a solution to break the back of addiction. All of what I have seen in these dreams and what the Lord has told me is foreign to me and very out there.

I told the Lord if He made a way we would go. We decided to sell everything we own. We put what we could fit in two cars and said our good byes and headed to California. We did not know anyone, had no housing set up or jobs. 100% Faith In The Calling!

We got all settled in our new city, it took some hardship, but God was adjusting our hearts as well. We were both able to find great jobs.

In my new job, as a drug and alcohol counselor in one of Redding's community health centers the Lord showed up so many times that it still blows me away. Many of my appointments that I had with my new clients were God encounters. He told me He needed me there to connect and help some of His children that had been crying out for help. He told me that this job was just to lay a foundation to get my name out in the community, to buy a home, and then He would release me to start The Counseling Center I had always dreamed about.

You would never guess, but in September of 2016 we bought a beautiful home on three acres. I planted five "Anointed Apricot Trees." We bought these trees when we were still renting in faith not even knowing that we would buy a house. This is an important part of my dream with Kris V. because I did not have a house, land, or apricot trees when I had the dream.

I put in my two-week notice. This was not planned. In my mind, because I liked it so much, I saw myself there a couple more years. I will not get into the details why, but a couple of days after I turned in my notice, I saw that I had been in a comfort zone the Lord wanted to get me out of, so we could get started on why He brought us to Redding, CA.

We found an office in downtown Redding and on Valentine's Day was the official start date of The Counseling Center. I am so stoked to see part of my longtime dream of opening a counseling center finally happening.

I am looking so forward to connecting with you via email/facebook/website. If the Lord would do it for me, He will surely do it for you.

Thank you so much for taking time to listen to some of my crazy story. I know a lot of this is not a normal story. Let me assure you, if you're in active addiction your story is not normal either.

I will be praying for you and believing for changes of greatness. Connect with us and tell us all the great changes the Lord is doing in your life. I will make you a 100% guarantee that if you practice the principles in this book daily you can't go back to allowing life controlling behaviors rule you.

chapter fourteen

HOW TO GET SOBER TODAY

Here are steps you can take today to get sober:

- Ask Jesus to come in and fill the empty void in your soul. Ask Him to forgive you of sin and help you to forgive those who sinned against you.

- Start a journal to use at the beginning or the end of each day and write about all the positive and negative feelings you had that day.

- Find a faith-based recovery meeting, like Celebrate Recovery or Overcomers, etc. NA and AA will do, if you cannot find a faith-based meeting.

- Find a local church that offers emotional healing and addictions counseling. Most churches offer these services free of charge.

- Find a good, solid, Bible-believing church to go to.

- Get a Bible you can understand and start reading the book of John.

- Identify whether you need to go to a detox facility. Some of these are state run and free of charge.

- Find a good Christian music station or go online. If you have a smart phone download Z88.3, they have Christian rap, rock and pop. I advise you to stay away from any music you listened to while getting high. Music is very powerful and can remind you of memories of getting high and the so called good times.

- Watch on TV only things that will add value to your life. (Remember you store every image you see and all things you hear.)

- Only read books that will add to you spiritually and for now stay away from novels and fantasy books that do not have a positive message.

- Stop talking to and hanging out with anyone that connects you to your life controlling behaviors. If you are living in an unhealthy environment, pray that God will open a door for you to get out.

- Call those you know that are living right and tell them your life is changing and you need positive people around you. Ask if they're willing to talk to you on the phone and hold you accountable. Go and do something together. We need others to help us.

- Make it known publicly, (i.e. Facebook) that you don't live like that anymore. Ask your friends to respect this and be prepared to delete them if need be.

- Get new phone number and delete all old numbers.

PART TWO

Becoming Addicted No More

WORKBOOK

ACKNOWLEDGEMENTS

Inspired by the flock of men I was so blessed to shepherd at one of the recovery programs I was part of. I was taking them through the Dunklin Inner Healing book, reading it out loud, and we all agreed that we needed to edit and create a more current version revolving around our own life experiences. I decided to edit this companion workbook. Although we started out doing the first two chapters in the book, with all of us giving our input, we soon realized that we all had differing opinions, and I, being a bit OCD, thought the best thing was for me just to do it alone. These men, however, are still so much a part of this and I want to send much love to them all. They are great men of God who are still walking the fine line of greatness, sometimes one step forward and two steps backward. I love you all and am thankful for the inspiration you gave me to edit this workbook. I couldn't have done this if it wasn't for my beautiful wife who continues to push me to write and has laid down her dreams that mine may be accomplished. The most selfless lady of Christ I know. Love you, Baby Girl!

ABOUT THE WORKBOOK

This idea was originally part of an inner healing book created from a faith-based recovery program called Dunklin Memorial Camp in Florida that was written many years ago. I personally walked men through that book. Over the years, I could see the value and importance of it for all people with life controlling issues and in dealing with the emotional pain it causes, and in turn, the pain caused to others. I was convinced that issues other than addictions needed to be faced, like control, unforgiveness, resentments, rejection, low self-esteem, anger, sexual abuse, and many others. I made the decision to edit the original book that would relate to all people, so this *edited workbook was created. I have used some things out of the original book, but some of it has been rewritten/edited. Some things were removed and added. I am grateful to the Dunklin staff who wrote it many years ago, to whom I credit this great work.

I received written permission via email from Dunklin's Vice President, Todd Haskell, on 12/1/2016 to use this edited version of their inner healing book.

*Inner Healing by Dunklin Memorial Camp, 1992

session one

MAKING SENSE OF IT ALL

Soul Healing is the healing of our inner person, which we refer to as our soul. Our soul consists of our mind, our will, and our emotions. Therefore, Soul Healing is healing of the mind, the will and the emotions.

We have learned that memories of the "good ole' fun times" tempts us to stay in or return to our life controlling behaviors, because it allows us to remember only the good things about our experiences within our behavior. Even though these memories are powerful, it is not the true reason we stay in or return to our behavior.

When we have inner hurts and damaged emotions because of what others have done to us and or what we have done to other people, we learned that the use of life controlling behaviors help us hide from these painful memories. For many of us this is the reason we continue to abuse substances. We are hiding from our emotional pain.

We will look at rejection, shame, physical abuse, mental abuse, sexual abuse, guilt, unworthiness, insecurity, and more. We will discuss how these issues have controlled our lives.

Soul Healing is a process. It is not an overnight cure for our problems. There are many different areas of Soul Healing. Soul Healing is part of becoming whole and healthy in the three major relationships of life, which are:

89

1. *Our relationship with God.*

2. *Our relationship with ourselves.*

3. *Our relationship with others.*

There are two major parts in the healing process. There is a part for which God is responsible, and there is part for which we are responsible. We cannot do God's part, and God will not do our part.

As we go through this process, we will take time to get deep into our mind, will and emotions. We will give God access to these deep areas of our lives. This is the only way that God will be able to change us.

Some of us have likely experienced some 'clean time' at some point in our lives, but have found it to be so painful we couldn't bear it. This means there are some things within us that only God can heal. These are things from which we need to be set free.

Soul Healing is a process which allows God to give us insight concerning certain problems in our lives that are related to past events that continue to affect our present and future. Through this process we will return to those events and allow them to surface so God can heal them.

We will not simply use our imagination; we will actually bring the Lord Jesus Christ into each past experience. We will allow Him to give us insight into the situation, and we will allow Him to heal us of the destructive things others have done or that we have done to others. God gave us a memory and we are to use it. We will come to realize that after we are healed and when the memories return, the hurt and the pain from those memories will no longer exist.

Memories will always be with us. Everything we have experienced has been stored in our soul like a computer's hard drive. Our problem is that things we have experienced in the past influence us in the present. They still hurt or bother us. It is as if we carry a sack full of old garbage around with us. If we have come from a broken home, or if we have life controlling behaviors, we probably have painful memories from the past. In all likelihood, we have damaged emotions.

One of the most common damaged emotions is the fear of rejection. We did not develop the fear of rejection when we decided to seek help; we probably had the fear of rejection before we started to have life controlling issues. Or, perhaps, because of these issues, we have allowed such fear to come in.

Some of the negative emotions we carry around with us may come from our life controlling issues, such as addiction, etc. On other hand, some of these emotions may have come from our childhood, before any life controlling issues took place. They could even be a combination of both.

As we woke up this morning, we carried many things over from the past into the present. There could be a memory of one particular event that seems to surface often. It could be something we have done, or something that someone has done to us. It could be the memory of an accident, death, divorce, or abuse of some kind.

Any memory that continues to surface may cause us some type of emotional discomfort. This is a sure sign that something is not right within us. These are the memories and emotions that we will bring before the Lord. We will allow Him to show us what we need to do with them.

Alone we are unable to make these memories go away, and we are unable to stop them from hurting. But if we allow the Lord to show us what to do with these memories/feelings/emotions, we will put ourselves in a position to receive healing from Him.

As we carry these emotions from day to day without dealing with them, they become part of us; therefore, we take them into tomorrow with us. There are very few of these feelings and emotions that time alone can heal. Time usually doesn't heal anything, it tends to make things worse. This is why we go deeper and deeper into our life controlling behaviors. Only meeting with the Lord about our past and meeting with Him daily can heal us.

Unless we are healed, those things which we have been carrying for a long period of time will cause us to react in certain ways towards ourselves and others. We need more than just time. Healing is a process and it will be accomplished by the Lord who can bring about complete healing, not simply relying on the passage of time.

The Bible says through the writer Paul, "Not that I have already attained, or am already perfect; but I press on, that I may lay hold of that for which Christ Jesus has laid hold of me. Brothers I do not count myself to have apprehended; but one thing I do, forgetting those things which are behind and reaching forward to those things ahead, I press toward the goal for the prize of the upward call of God in Christ Jesus." (Phil. 3:12-14 NKJV)

This says that Paul is standing in the present today. In the first part of this verse Paul makes it clear that he has not arrived, that he is not yet what he wants to become; that he doesn't have it all put together. He understands that he must constantly be putting all things behind him, not necessarily forgetting them, but practicing the ongoing process of leaving things in the past.

Paul is not talking about an absence of being able to recall, he is talking about laying aside the things that are behind him. Paul had a bad past; he was a lot like us in that respect. When the Lord got Saul's (who was later named Paul) attention on the road to Damascus, he probably felt a lot of guilt and shame because he had been part of a group that was imprisoning and killing Christians, all in the name of the Lord.

Paul may not have had a drug or alcohol problem, but he had some issues in the past, which gave him emotional pain and hurt, and he had to deal with them. He had to get right with God and receive God's forgiveness. He realized the need to lay those things aside in order to go on with his life. He did not ignore them and stuff them deep down into his emotional boxes and say they never happened.

Ignoring something is not the same as being healed of that thing. Ignoring is not healing. Each incident must be dealt with, then it can laid behind and will no longer bother us.

The problem is we don't readily deal with painful events. We repress them in our emotions with the hope that if we don't think of them they will not bother us, or they will go away. But the truth is we do think about them, and they never go away. Each time the memories return we push them back down. This process is repeated over and over again, and this leaves us hurting and dying on the inside.

Paul also said that at the same time he lays those things behind him, he reaches forward and presses on. He is not just pushing things back down on the inside; he is dealing with them and pressing on.

Do you see the truth that Paul has grasped? He is focusing on the present. We call this, "three way thinking," or "three dimensional thinking," and it is very necessary for us to develop. As Paul stands in the present, he can look at the past. He makes a decision to put some past things aside, so he can work in the present which will affect his future.

Because he is able to do this, his future will be different from his past. He no longer allows the events of the past to affect him with their negative influences.

It is the same with us. If we don't work today on our relationship with God and allow Him to work in us, we will awaken tomorrow morning with the same undealt with emotions of today. But if we allow God to change us today, our future will be different from our past.

The opposite of three way thinking is "one way thinking" or "one dimensional thinking." A good example of a one way thinker is the person who writes a bad check. They know there is no money in the bank to cover the check, but they think one way, they are not concerned about the future. They may even write more than one bad check. They don't look at the past and learn from it. When we are one way in our thinking, we see no further than the end of our noses. Our main thought is, "I want what I want, and I want it now!!"

We become like the mule the farmer puts blinders on so he can only see in front of himself; we can see in one direction only. We are only interested in what we are going to get today and how we are going to get it. I like to call it suffering from "First Thought Wrong."

Because we are one way thinkers, we repeat the same mistakes in our lives over and over again. We will make a mess of our lives, leave it, and go somewhere else and make another mess just like the first one, never learning from the past and never looking to the future.

But all these messes hurt us and others. They have caused us problems. After we receive healing and have been set free from our life controlling issues a while, we begin to remember the things we did and the things we said. It is at this time, if we are open to it, the Holy Spirit puts His hand upon us and brings those things to the surface to be dealt with.

Like Paul, we have to start laying these issues (our past) aside. We have to deal with them once and for all and go on to God's plan and purpose for our lives. We can't carry bags of garbage with us the rest of our lives because they will destroy us. They will generate an opposing reaction and response to every area and experience in our lives.

Can you imagine what it would be like if we never emptied our garbage can? What if we did nothing but press down the new garbage on top of the old? It wouldn't be long until we would be unable to get near the garbage can because of how bad the smell was.

That is what is happening inside of us. That is why many of us react the way we do and why others react to us the way they do. The garbage inside us stinks. God wants to clean it up; God wants to heal us. And we can be healed, but only through giving Jesus Christ access to our soul (mind, will, and emotions). It is impossible to heal ourselves. Soul

Healing reaches beneath the surface problems of our life controlling behaviors. There may be many issues in our lives, but God will take care of all of them, if we will let Him.

It is possible for us to have been in recovery for a period of months, and to feel much better physically than when we started , yet continue to be tired and worn out on the inside, because of the empty void. Jesus offers us hope through an invitation to resolve these feelings. Jesus says in the Bible, "Are you tired or (weary)? Worn out? Burned out on religion? Come to me. Get away with me and you will recover your life (and find rest in your soul). I'll show you how to take a real rest (in your soul). Walk with me and work with me—watch how I do it. Learn the unforced rhythms of grace (unmerited favor). I won't put anything heavy (laden) or ill-fitting on you. Keep company with me and you'll learn freely and lightly." (Matthew 11:28-30 MSG; parenthesis, NKJV)

Jesus said we would find rest for our soul through Him. We have learned that our soul is our mind, will, and emotions. That is what is weary and heavy in us. That is where we are hurting, and the only way the soul can be healed is through the Spirit of God. God is the one who sets us free.

Jesus is ready to heal our inside soul pain, as well as any healing in our body. Suppose we cut our foot some time ago, but it has since healed. We can look at the foot and remember the pain as if it was yesterday, but the foot doesn't hurt anymore because it has healed.

That is physical healing. The same principle applies to the mind, will, and emotions. For our foot to heal, we had to do certain things. The doctor may have told us not to get the foot wet. If it got wet and it became infected, we had to go back to the doctor. The doctor reopened the wound and re-stitched it. Eventually, the foot healed. It took time; it didn't happen the next day. It may have taken as long as a year. The memory of this event may return often, but it isn't painful because the foot is healed. It was important that we followed the doctor's orders because the infection could have caused us to have the foot cut off or may have even killed us.

That is the process we are facing as we let God heal our inner wounds and damaged emotions. It is important for us to see the process in the relationship between the outer person and the inner person, where healing is concerned. God can heal our damaged emotions, so that when the memory of the issue surfaces, there will be no more pain. The damage has been healed, even though the memory is still there.

Our natural reaction has been to stuff our hurts in to the deepest parts of our souls (mind, will, and emotions). Now we need to learn how to allow these things to surface. We need to look at them and give God access to them. This is very important. Once we have experienced God's healing in our lives, the fear of allowing these damaged emotions to surface will be destroyed. Until we experience this, we will have a fear of coming before the Lord with our emotions.

Our first order of business was and still is to deal with our present emotions daily, and then we can start looking at the past. We have to learn to lay the past behind us. Unless we do, we will continue to carry our past garbage into the present, which in turn will continue to affect our future.

Let's look at a few things that start creating an unhealthy Soul.

We are born into relationships that have had breaks. How do we get breaks in our relationships? We can look and see that most of these breaks start right in the home at a very early age. Any home which does not have God first is dysfunctional. Every dysfunctional home experiences breaks in relationships. The breaks occur when something is said to us or done to us that cause emotional wounds.

For instance, our parents, foster parents, friends or family members, or others may have told us that we were no good, or we would never amount to anything. Such a statement from someone whose opinion we respect causes a break. Lack of attention or lack of encouragement also causes a break. Rejection is a major break, and so is abandonment. Any kind of abuse whether verbal, physical, mental or sexual, will always cause a break in relationship.

It is natural for us to try to recover from those breaks. We try to build a bridge back to our need for love, acceptance, and forgiveness. Some of us have attempted to use addiction or some other life controlling behavior as our recovery program from the breaks in our relationships. Because we have received so many wounds in our lives, we have attempted to medicate these wounds with many different life controlling behaviors.

In our attempt in doing this, we have been led to believe that we have found some worthiness, some security, and some peace. We have disconnected in our relationships because of what has been said or done to us and what we have said and done to others. Through choosing to deal with these life controlling issues, we are really trying to become reconnected to the relationships God has called us to be in from birth.

Adoption, for example, often leaves a child with the emotion of rejection. This can go all the way back to when the child was in its mother's womb. That feeling of being rejected is a deep emotional wound that is still there, even though the baby may have been put into a loving home with loving parents.

This rejection is always present, and it continually motivates the emotionally wounded person to try to re-establish that break in their relationship. It is a wound that must be healed. The attempt to reconnect starts immediately after the break, and continues until it is dealt with and healed.

It is important for us to understand that even as a child, when we have these breaks in our relationships, we will often turn to something that will give us a sense of belonging, a sense of acceptance, a sense of security which we could not get from home.

There is something about participating in our life controlling behaviors, perhaps it is the environment, or perhaps it is being accepted, which re-establishes a connection with something we long for. What most of us have been trying to do is get reconnected. Unfortunately, we have chosen a substitute way, which will never fulfill our need or fill that empty hole/void that continues to burn deep inside of each of us.

The truth is God is the only one to Whom we have to get connected. Our relationship with God is our first step. At the same time we must look back and examine those things that have been driving us, and understand how they have affected us.

Some of the things that have caused disconnections may have been small. Perhaps they were destructive affirmations or never hearing a word of encouragement, things not said at a time when we really needed to hear them. These may seem like little things, but at the time, in the life of a five-year-old, twenty-five-year-old or a sixty-five-year-old they could have made a major impact. Such incidents can easily cause disconnections.

One of the main things we discover about our life controlling behaviors is that in using them we could feel good, even if it was only for a little while. We could place ourselves in a fantasy world in which we could be accepted and escape the emotions that were damaged. Our relationships were fantasy, but at least they were relationships, and that was acceptable to us.

Those of us who have grown up without a father or mother, or perhaps without either parent, have been disconnected from the start from what God intended for us. That doesn't mean we can justify attempting to reconnect through turning to life controlling behaviors.

We need to understand that God has made a way to reconnect these breaks. We may not have an earthly father, but we certainly have a heavenly Father. Unfortunately, a five-, twenty-five-, or sixty-five-year-old may not realize God has made a way to reconnect these breaks.

We will be looking at certain events that have cause disconnections in our lives. A slap across the face is easier to take than a damaging cut with the tongue. The slap hurts less and for a shorter period of time. Damage done by the tongue and undealt with will stay with us a life time as a damaged emotion. How do we know this? Because this very moment you can think about the damage done and still feel the hurt it caused you. This contributes to the way we have been living.

Physical abuse is a big problem as well, but even bigger is what has been done to us by what has been said to us and what we have said and done to others. We have lived most of our lives with these restrictive barriers. Many of us have become the exact words spoken against us and many have become the words we spoke to them. We have acted out what we believed about ourselves.

As we go through this Soul Healing course we will dive deep into the root of what our problems really are. We will find that we don't have a problem with life controlling behaviors; this has just been our way of dealing with our emotions without God and trying to reconnect the breaks in our relationships.

I am very blessed and honored that you have opened a door for help and chosen to be healthy and whole in your relationship to God, Yourself, and Others.

Keep your head up; God has a great plan and purpose for your life!

Questions

1. Why is it difficult for those with an unhealthy soul to stop their life controlling behaviors?

2. In what ways do painful memories have an effect on our lives?

3. Why is important for us to lay behind our past and focus on the present?

4. Describe one-way thinking and three-way thinking.

5. Describe what is meant by a break in our relationships?

6. Why is it Important for us to reconnect these breaks?

7. Can you relate your current life controlling behaviors to things that have happened in your past? (Yes__ or No__)

8. If Yes, are you willing to bring these issues before yourself, anoth er, and God so that you may receive healing in these areas? (Yes__ or No__)

9. What do you feel is the first thing you need to do to start this healing process?

10. Record any thoughts or feelings that you can relate to in this ses sion, and what you learned about yourself.

session two

BROKEN

Many people come from broken relationships and broken homes. That doesn't necessarily mean you will turn to life controlling behaviors like addiction. Addiction is just another form of dysfunction. As we said before any home in which Christ is not the Head is broken and dysfunctional.

Verbal abuse, physical abuse, sexual abuse, or even a highly demanding parent can produce dysfunction in a home. The parent who requires constant perfection creates a climate of performance in the home. The child is prompted to perform to receive love and attention. This is a dysfunctional atmosphere.

David in the Bible says, "Oh yes, you shaped me first inside, then out; you formed me in my mother's womb. I thank you God—You're breathtaking! Body and soul, I am marvelously made! I worship in adoration—what a creation! You know me inside out, you know my every bone in my body, and you know exactly how I was made, bit by bit, how I was sculpted from nothing into something. Like an open book, you watched me grow from conception to birth; all the stages of my life were spread out before you, the days of my life all prepared before I'd even lived one day." (Psalm 139:13-16 MSG)

In this passage of Scripture, David talks about being formed in our mother's womb. God formed our inward parts. God created us. There is a very important sense of connection while we are in our mother's womb. Of course, there is a physical connection through the umbilical cord, but there is also another connection. It is in the form of love, security, and acceptance. This connection provides a feeling that all is well.

There is a study that has been done that proves this is true for all babies. If they are not shown love, if they are not touched and cuddled, they will die. As a matter of fact, that can happen even in the womb, when babies are unwanted. This is called Marasmus. It is a gradual and continuous wasting away of the body. Marasmus proves there is a definite need within us for connectedness.

Some of us were born into connected relationships. Unless there is the threat of abortion or adoption while we were in the womb, we probably felt connected and would have a sense of love, security, and acceptance.

As our lives unfold, we experience situations that bridge or connect us to people. One very important bridge is the act of touching. The act of touch brings an extra dimension into the relationship. Touching is a bridge that connects people. Also, when we feel secure and accepted in the presence of others, that bridges us to them. It tightens our relationship, and promotes connectedness.'

Often, our bridges of connection with people become broken. Sometimes they are repaired, but many times they are not. For instance, our father or mother may have disciplined or spanked us because we did something they told us not to do. During the spanking there was probably a lot of fear, hurt and anger in us.

The bridge between our father or mother may have been temporarily broken. But after they disciplined us, if they sat down and said I love you and explained why they disciplined you, that broken bridge was repaired.

Some of our broken bridges are repaired in that fashion. In early childhood we tend to experience broken bridges easily, but some of those breaks are merely hairline fractures. Such breaks can usually be repaired with a kind word and a hug. The problem comes when we experience a broken bridge that does not get repaired.

Breaks of this type disconnect us from the assurance of security and acceptance and love that we need. If our father or mother or another tells us we are useless; we are nothing but a burden; and they would be better off if they never had us; this would have created a deep break. With such a break, all our connections and our feelings of security, love and acceptance leave immediately.

Breaks of this type can produce guilt, shame, fear, anger, and many other negative emotions. When bridges are broken in this manner and never repaired, the disconnection from love and security begins to widen. Many times this causes us to react by trying to repair the bridge that has been broken through things like over-achievement, performance, and life controlling behaviors like addiction, overeating, wrong sexual desire, anger and many others things like these. We begin to act out and do things to get attention because we have been disconnected.

We were deeply wounded by things that were said and done to us or what we did or said to others in our meaningful relationships. As a result, we reach out, and do whatever we can to make these relationships work. We are trying to restore what should be there naturally, but that bridge has been broken. We can no longer trust those who have caused the break and many times others can no longer trust us when we have caused a break.

At this point, fear can creep into us. We may feel shame and unworthiness. When someone says, "You're never going to amount to anything," that statement inflicts a deep wound and unfortunately the break is never repaired unless you or the person who said this to you apologizes and says, "I was wrong, I never should have said that. I love you and you are going to amount to something."

If that repair is not made, our belief system kicks in, and the destructive statements that they have said or that we have said to them becomes a part of them and us. We begin to believe what was told to us, we begin to feel they were right, and begin to behave as if it is a fact.

As this process continues to grow, we begin to feel guilty about the things we should do but aren't doing. We may even begin to feel responsible for the things that are happening in our lives.

Our emotions take over and we start to get very upset with how we have become. We ask ourselves questions, such as, "Why couldn't I have had a family or life like normal people? Why don't my daddy and mommy love me like Jason's daddy loves him? Why do my parents have to be addicts and alcoholics?"

We feel miserable. We have lost the connection that is very necessary to us. God created us with that need built in. After the disconnection, we do not deliberately look for addictions or life controlling behaviors as the answer. We look for any way we can find to be reconnected. We want what we were designed to have; what we had before the breaks. We search for the intimacy of a meaningful relationship. We long for the trust, love and acceptance we had before the bridge was broken.

As we continue this search, many of us try different life controlling behaviors as a way to reconnect, be accepted and loved. Doing these gives a false feeling of worthiness. When we are under the influence of our substance of choice, we enter fantasyland. We see ourselves as we wish we were instead of as we really are. We also see situations as we wish they were instead of as they are.

This way of dealing with our emotions medicates our pain. Through this distorted process, we are really trying to get back to where we were safely connected, the place for which God created us. This is our failed attempt to restore breaks in our relationships without God's help.

It is easy to see that the more disconnected we are, the more dysfunctional we become. Also, the further our disconnection becomes, the more we try to reconnect. As we fall into life controlling behaviors our actions become more and more bizarre.

We are still trying to re-establish something that is missing, something that God meant for us to have. What we don't understand is that reconnection can only begin when we come to God. Reconnection cannot begin in relationships with other people. We have to get into a deep relationship with God.

Reconnection begins through Salvation. It begins at the time we invite Jesus Christ into our heart to fill the empty void. After the reconnection process is underway, there are still life controlling behavior patterns that we have to deal with. This is true even though we have received Jesus. We still have to work with the life controlling behaviors that have become part of our lifestyle.

When we receive Christ, our life controlling behaviors are not immediately eliminated. This is why we need to begin to reconnect those broken bridges. Everyone who experiences a relationship break must go through this process if they want healing and wholeness.

Although we have been trying to recover from the hurts, wounds and the disconnections in our relationships, the first thing we need to recover from is our life controlling behaviors. We have to recover from what we have used and hoped would be the solution to our undealt with or broken/damaged emotions.

After we have dealt with our life controlling behaviors, then we will be freed from the guilt and shame and be ready to return to the point at which our breaks took place and deal with them effectively. We will not be able to deal with them while still addicted and afflicted with these life controlling behaviors.

There is a difference between guilt and shame. Guilt relates to behavior, while shame relates to identity. Guilt says, "I made a mistake," but shame says, "I am a mistake." Shame is a powerful influence that has been controlling most of us for too long.

Many addictions and life controlling behaviors are shame based. If you were told you were a mistake or told someone they were a mistake and accepted it as truth, that broke a bridge and established a shame based emotion. Rejection, unworthiness, insecurity, low self-esteem and many like emotions are all issues that stem from bridges of relationships that were broken or bridges that we never established that were meant to be.

If we were told we are no good or said that to someone, our immediate emotional reaction was, "If I'm no good, maybe I'm not loved and not going to be protected." That reveals an area of our lives in which our security has been taken from us. We then, from a very early age, attempt to recover that broken bridge; we are actually trying to recapture our security.

As we begin our Soul Healing and restoring of relationships, there is something we must understand: If we want the Lord to work in our past, we must be willing to let God work in the present. We must be open and willing to being restored in our present circumstances before we can expect to go back and be reconciled to past events.

We will not be able to resolve the break that happened ten years ago if we can't resolve something that happened today. This is why we start the healing with the recording and dealing with our emotions daily so that we do not store any more garbage in our emotions that are not going to benefit us.

Broken bridges are very serious emotional wounds. Because of this, we need to allow the Lord to show us the breaks in our lives. We probably have forgotten some of the things that were said or done to cause the breaks. God will reveal them to us as we ask Him. We have most likely packed down most of these incidents. We should begin today and ask God to reveal them to us.

An estimated ninety-five percent of those who seek healing had a poor relationship with one or both parents. They may lack in any healthy parent relationship. It may not entirely be the fault of the parent, but that really isn't important at this point.

It doesn't matter whose fault it is. Our purpose is not to find fault, our purpose is to receive healing. To accomplish that, we have to bring these breaks in our relationships to the Lord and let Him heal these damaged emotions.

Sometimes we cannot reconnect with someone, because that person is not open to us or is no longer living. But we can reconnect to and through God. We can't change other people, but God will show us how to love and forgive them right where they are. God will give us His insight and His wisdom concerning our broken relationships.

We may still desire a close, intimate relationship with a certain person, but that is sometimes impossible because of the attitude or condition of the other person. However, God can still heal those hurts and wounds of the past. He will make the reconnection possible from our end, even if the other person is not open to it.

Not all relationships can be restored, but all emotional wounds inside us can be healed. We may never be able to have the close relationship we want with certain people, but we will discover that we no longer have to carry around the hurts and the wounds that we caused or suffered from that relationship.

As we bring these things before the Lord, He will allow us to begin to understand ourselves and the people we've hurt and those who have hurt us. Understanding someone is not the same as forgiving them, but understanding helps give us insight as to why something may have happened. That is an important part of the healing process. It is much easier to forgive and be set free when we understand more about others, about ourselves and God's principles.

Actually, that is what healing is all about. Forgiveness is the key to healing. The Bible says, "For if you forgive the failures of others, your heavenly Father will also forgive you. But if you don't forgive others, then your Father will not forgive your failures." (Matthew 6:14-15 GW)

When we are unwilling to forgive, we are reserving the right to get even. God is unable to forgive us until we are willing to forgive others and seek forgiveness ourselves. Forgiveness is a spiritual law from which we cannot escape. Like the law of gravity, "What goes up, must come down." If we judge others, the very same things we see in them that we dislike, will be repeated in us until we forgive.

Let's look at an example of a broken bridge with a spouse. The wife finds out the husband is actively involved in addiction to drugs. As addiction breaks the marriage, the woman naturally looks for reconnection. In the process she becomes a classic enabler. She begins to behave in a way she believes will bring intimacy back into the marriage.

The bridge is broken because the husband is out of the home often drugging and now he is having sex as well. The addiction that the husband has is just his attempt at the recovery process of his own damaged emotions. He tries to medicate the pain he feels, the loneliness, the depression, the rejection, the unworthiness and the shame.

The wife, who has now become co-dependent, has the same feelings as her husband. She feels shame, guilt, anger, rejection, betray, and abandonment. Her attempt at recovery is to try to solve all the problems. Her behaviors become erratic as she attempts to fix her husband so she can reconnect the broken bridge.

There is a major danger in co-dependency and life controlling behaviors. Sometimes the one trying to reconnect can fall into the same type of behaviors themselves as a way to deal with the breaks or they both may look to other relationships. They may try a substitute relationship, thinking if they connect to a new person they can regain what they had before the break.

Those who have been in a relationship with those struggling with life controlling behaviors continue to seek the, "all is well" connection. They may continue to seek relationships and life controlling behaviors with the hope that they will feel reconnected. Of course that will never work. It will always lead back to the same empty void. The reconnection process can only begin with the acceptance of Jesus Christ.

As we end session two, remember, starting today, that what we say and do to others will last a lifetime in that person and us. Words are powerful and can bring life or death. Most of all the undealt with emotions are from words. Today make a commitment to say what will help others not what will hurt them. God has a great plan and purpose for your life. Don't give up on yourself, because God will never leave or of forsake you!

Questions

1. Write with as much detail as possible, a hurtful event that occurred in your past. Describe who hurt you, where you were hurt, how old you were, etc. Then deter-mine that person's responsibility and what your part was in it.

2. Describe a broken bridge.

3. If an important bridge was broken, how does that affect us?

4. Why is important for us to lay behind our past and focus on the present?

5. Why do we choose life controlling behaviors like addiction as a method to repair the broken bridge?

6. What is the only way reconnection can begin for you?

7. What does God say about forgiving other's faults, and what does He expect from you?

session three

REJECTED

Rejection and the fear of rejection is another set of damaged emotions that play a major part in the development of the character of every human being.

The Bible talks about how damaged emotions affect us. Here are a few examples:

> "A joyful heart makes a cheerful face, but when the heart is sad, the spirit is broken." (Proverbs 15:13 NASB) (One of the products of rejection is a broken spirit.)

> "A joyful heart is good medicine, but a broken spirit dries up the bones." (Proverbs 17:22 NASB) (A broken spirit, brought about by rejection is capable of drying up, or taking away the desire for life.)

> "The spirit of a man can endure his sickness, but a broken spirit who can bear?" (Proverbs 18:14 NASB) (If the desire for life has gone, there is no chance for healing to take place.)

Even Jesus Himself was despised and rejected, a man of sorrows, and acquainted with deepest grief. This paints a picture of the Lord understanding what we are going through because He went through it, so He is able to help us through it. Because He loves us and endured these emotions, we may be free of them.

The most powerful positive emotional force in the universe is the love of God. The Bible says, "The one who does not love does not k now God, for God is love. And we have come to know and have believed the love which God has for us. God is love and the one who abides in love abides in God, and God abides in him." (I John 4:8;16 NASB) (God is love; therefore, love is God's most powerful force.)

If love is the most powerful force in creation, it follows that lack of love is the most powerful negative force in creation.

Rejection is the denial of love and acceptance in our lives. It is probably the most painful, the most neglected, yet one of the most common emotional wounds from which we suffer.

There are many forms of rejection—from words said to us, to abuse done to us, or the words and abuse we have done to others. This knowledge does not make it easy to recognize. We keep these rejected feelings closely hidden deep in our emotional boxes and have indulged in life controlling behaviors as a defense action to protect us from the emotional feeling of rejection and other like feelings.

God designed us in such a way that we cannot function properly without dealing with these emotions and accepting His love and His way of doing things. Our survival in life depends upon it. His love is the one ingredient each of us needs in order to grow, to flourish, and to become the people we need to be so that we can fulfill the purpose for which God created us. Love is to us as water and sunshine is to a flower. It is necessary for our growth. If we don't understand that each of us needs to be loved, we walk on dangerous ground. Because each of us needs love, we each desire it strongly. We were created to be loved and accepted, so if we don't have this we will slowly die on the inside, which will in effect, kill the outside.

God created us to fellowship with Him, to worship Him, and to have relationship with Him. Love is the primary ingredient in that relationship. Love is God's motive, and it should be our motive as well. Throughout the Bible, God's love is always evident. Whether we realize it or not, God loves us.

When we are in true relationship with God, His love for us creates within us an ability to love one another. According to Jesus, the two greatest commandments are to love God, and to love one another. Love is the fuel that makes us function. It nourishes us and gives us meaning in life. Without love, we develop serious problems. When we are denied love and the attention we need, we experience emotional affliction.

As we mature in our relationship with God and learn to deal with our emotions, most of us start to handle rejection better than we could before. We are like a palm tree in that respect. If we plant a small palm tree, it needs a lot of water, sun and fertilizer. It must have more attention while it is small and growing. Once it has grown, it can withstand the cold and the storms, but when it was small and young it could not handle the abuse. We are just like that.

Many of us today react from the wounds of rejection we gave to others and ones we received ourselves. We find that many times we still can't handle rejection. This is because most of us were wounded at an early age, and we have been reacting through those wounds ever since.

Emotional wounds are very painful. Nothing hurts quite like being rejected. When we are not accepted, when we are looked down upon or not loved, we experience deep emotional pain. Once we have experienced rejection, we react by building protective walls in our soul (mind, will, and emotions). We begin to lead a life that guards against the possibility of ever being rejected again, due to the hurt, anger and pain it causes.

We can look at the way we act towards rejection in the same way we treat a sprained arm. Everything we do revolves around that injury. We don't want to hurt it again and feel that pain once more, so we are very careful to protect it. This form of self-protection is a natural reaction to any kind of physical injury.

We treat emotional wounds in the same manner. Every response in every relationship that is negative revolves around our past and present emotional wounds in a way that protects us from experiencing the hurts again. The result is that, as a wounded person, we behave in a dysfunctional manner. We become unstable in our attitudes and our relationships, and many times turn to life controlling behaviors as a way to cope with these emotions.

The question always is, "How has that been working for us?"

It is time we deal with these emotions once and for all so that we can be all that God has called us to be, and that time is now, today!

Most deep wounds started when we were young children. Children often misinterpret correction or lack of attention as rejection. It may not have been intended as rejection, but that doesn't matter. If that is how we saw it and felt about it, that is how we reacted to it.

Even today many of us cannot tell the difference between correction and rejection. We take correction as rejection; because that is the way it makes us feel, whether or not the rejection actually took place doesn't matter. What matters is that we think it does, and many times we react with the negative emotion of rejection.

We are wounded by what is said or done to us, even though it may be done out of love. We may find ourselves very sensitive during the first stages of our recovery. As someone corrects us, we may become devastated because we take it as rejection.

If we have accepted this wound of rejection into our emotions it creates one of two paths. The first is a fear of further rejection. Once we are wounded, we run from the act of being wounded again. For instance, if someone who is an authority figure in our lives has wounded us through rejection, our natural reaction is to fear authority and to guard ourselves when we are around authority figures.

For example, our incorrect concept of God almost always comes from the relationship we had with an authority figure in our lives, such as our father, mother or someone else in our lives. If we are not able to work through these emotions, we will carry that wrong concept throughout our lives.

The fear of additional hurt causes us to put up defense mechanisms. We begin to ask ourselves, "Who can I trust? Will the ones who I caused or caused me to suffer in the past hurt me again? Will I hurt others or will others hurt me again?" We develop a distrust of everyone's motives and everyone we've hurt does the same towards us. This becomes a never ending cycle leading to try to somewhat deal with these, and that is the life controlling behaviors that we continue to lean on.

One word for such feelings is paranoid. We feel that everyone is out to hurt us and make us feel less than. We can't trust anyone. The root behind this emotional feeling is the fear of rejection. It is the fear of not being accepted, not being part of something, not being loved. The paranoid rejected person lives in constant torment without some type of substance or life controlling behavior to lean on. We will always react based on our current emotional belief system that is in place through the storage of undealt with emotions.

The other path that happens most is self-rejection. After we have accepted rejection in our lives for any long period of time, we begin to reject ourselves. We actually believe we are unworthy and unacceptable by others. We are fully convinced that we don't fit in or measure up, that we are not even fit as a human in the world. This belief causes us to personally reject ourselves. Very often this will show up strongly in our relationship with God, unable to receive that He loves us.

Both the fear of rejection and self-rejection control our behavior. Rejection is probably the most common damaged emotion and severe problem human beings face. Everyone who recognizes their need for emotional healing has experienced some type of rejection. Many of us have wounded others and have been wounded over and over again. This eventually produces self-rejection.

The more rejection we receive, the more rejected we feel, and the more we believe we deserve to be rejected. Many times we ask ourselves what is it about ourselves that cause others to reject us. Rejection from a loved one will make us think we are unacceptable or unworthy. We can handle not being liked by someone we don't know, but when we receive rejection from someone we love the hurt goes deep. This helps convince us we are unacceptable failures.

If we see ourselves as failures we try desperately to change. We try becoming someone acceptable, someone other than whom we really are. We think different, act different, and believe if we were someone else, we would be loved and accepted.

After looking at this we start to see that the key to enjoying acceptance by others is to become different from whom we are outside of God's plan for our life. We continue to seek to change our personality and become someone different, so we can have the love and acceptance we need. We begin to pattern ourselves after a fantasy in our own mind that many times leads us to many life controlling behaviors (addictions, etc.).

In reality all we are doing is trying to reconnect the many broken bridges that have occurred over the span of our entire lives. Without exception, all of us attempt to recover the peace, love, affirmation, confirmation and acceptance that were lost through our broken bridges. Through our life controlling behaviors we try to reconnect these breaks.

Let's talk about some of the negative emotions rejection and self-rejection brings us.

Hurt: There is pain inside us. Because we hurt, we feel that we have done everything wrong. We are to blame, and there is no place to turn to make the hurt go away, except for life controlling behaviors.

Self-Pity: This is the "the poor little me" syndrome. We become very aware of our insufficiencies and the fact that no one seems to understand or care what is happening to us.

Despair: Another word for despair is hopelessness. When we have totally rejected ourselves, we can't see ourselves as capable of being loved by others.

Depression: When we have been rejected and have rejected ourselves, we will always have a spirit of depression in us. We have believed the lie that we are useless. Depression becomes a very thick wall around us that doesn't come down easily. Thanks to God that He is not challenged by this and He will set us free when we give Him access to these negative emotions.

Suicide: If no one will miss us or cares for us, then why should we? Suicide becomes the ultimate withdrawal. We become so desperate we create a death wish as the only true way to deal with our emotions. We believe if we die everything will be fixed. What we don't realize is that suicide is the ego trip. We are totally "turned in" at this point; our total attention is on self (aka) Me, Me, and Me. We have become our own god, even to the point of making the decision in our lives of the time of our own death.

As we observe rejection from others and self-rejection, we can see two personalities reacting in different ways as they are exposed to rejection. One personality is mostly aggressive, while the other is becoming lifeless. It is not uncommon for us to move from one path to the other.

Many of us become very critical and judgmental when we have experienced rejection. The pathway of the fear of rejection creeps in over time, because of the many years of feeling rejected. This fear of rejection is always aggressive. Anger and resentment dominate us. On this path we are more prone to overdose or to be killed in an accident.

On the other hand, the pathway of self-rejection displays a personality that is generally beat down. On this path we are more prone to suicide. There is always hope for those who are on either pathway.

As we walk through emotional healing, we will always draw to what God says to us about our need to understand the importance of our relationship with Him. God is love. That means He loves us. We may have hurt people we love and people we love may have hurt us, and we may have experienced many broken bridges, breaks that have devastated us. But we now have God, and God tells us He wants us to "Cast all our cares on Him for He cares for us." (1 Peter 5:7)

Understanding these breaks in our lives helps us recognize our need for healing and wholeness. But emotional healing is beyond our capability; there is no way we can heal ourselves. Only Jesus can heal us permanently as we learn to bring the past, present, and future breaks in our relationships to Him. Once we realize this, our next step is to look at our responsibility in these breaks.

As we reach this point, it is time to ask ourselves who has felt rejection more than anyone else in the world? We don't have to look any further that Jesus Christ. He has felt what we have felt, and much more.

Now let's think about this: If we have many problems in our lives that stem from being rejected or rejecting others, who should we look to for help with them? Naturally, we would look to someone who had been through a similar problem. Jesus has certainly been through rejection, because He experienced and endured the ultimate rejection.

To get Jesus in our emotional hurts and wounds, we need to get in touch with those hurts and wounds. We need to take a hard look at what we have caused and what we have personally experienced. We want to look at the losses in our lives, the loss of love, the deep hurts, and the wounds of rejection that we have caused and that were done to us.

Our lives and those of others have been orchestrated and directed by our reactions to those wounds we have caused others and the ones we have received. We need healing in those areas, those specific events in our lives in which we caused and received rejection. We need healing whether the wounds we caused or the wounds that were inflicted were intentional or not.

The process, in which we get healing, is to say, "Lord, this specific incident I have written down still hurts me. I am hurting, Lord. I need your help. I give this to you right now. Please take it from me."

Questions

1.   To give healing a try we want you to take one incident of rejection in your life that was done to you or that you done to another, and write down all the details.

2.   Share it with another believer, and ask the Lord to help you with that wound of rejection. Ask Him to show you the root and the fruit that has come out of this rejection. Talk about what has come from the wound, what your reaction has been and how it has affected your life and the lives around you. Write down all your findings from this assignment.

3. Why do emotional wounds we received continue to affect us today?

4. Why is self-rejection so destructive?

5. Why do we try to act like someone other than who we really are?

6. What causes rejection even more the physical abuse?

7. Why is it important for us to take a hard look at what we have experienced through these emotional wounds and hurts?

session 4

THE FRUIT OF EMOTIONAL
HURTS AND WOUNDS

Emotional hurts and wounds act like trees with bitter roots. They can only produce bitter fruit. Listed below are some examples of this bitter fruit.

Inability to receive love:

When someone who is significant in our lives has rejected us or we have rejected others, it makes us and them feel unworthy. This establishes a root belief that we or they are unworthy, unloved; therefore, we are unable to receive love.

Inability to love others:

The root of being rejected by others destroys our ability to trust others. We are very carefully guarded when it comes to allowing ourselves to get into close relationships with others. If we cannot get close to another person then we cannot truly consider loving that person in a healthy manner.

Insecurity:

Because we have experienced rejection by someone significant in our lives, we don't know who we can trust. Deep down we are walking around on egg shells. We always expect betrayal or criticism to be right around the corner.

Withdrawal:

Because we feel this way in the presence of others, we feel there is safety in isolation. Many times we turn to life controlling behaviors like addiction to deal with these emotions. Then our natural tendency is to withdraw from society and the world around us and to focus on the world within us.

Suspicion:

Our inability to trust others breeds suspicion of everyone. We never really know when we might be wounded, hurt, or rejected again.

Less than:

Because we feel unworthy, we naturally feel less than to others. This less than feeling is reflected in our relationships and actions.

Social shyness:

Social gatherings are painful to us because we feel we are surrounded by people that are better than us, who look upon us as we look upon ourselves. Although this is not true, our mindset will not allow us to think differently.

Fear of failure:

We are convinced we are incapable of accomplishing anything as well as others can accomplish them. Our low expectation of ourselves is usually reflected in our willingness to stay in jobs or relationships that require little of us.

Fear of man:

Because we think everyone else is better than ourselves, we rarely do anything on our own for fear of being rejected and criticized. We prefer to be told what to do, when and how to do it. Our only problem from that point is following directions accurately.

Fear of rejection:

The fear of rejection keeps us from being our real selves. We are always in a performance mode, hoping to please others.

Daydreaming and fantasizing:

Because we fear reality, we do everything we can to escape it through life controlling behaviors. We are safe in the world of fantasy, never challenged, always victorious. This is our way of dealing with our emotions outside a relationship with God. Living in this daydreaming world can only generate an unhealthy personality.

Some reasons why we may have these emotional responses, or fruits; Parent rejections:

1. Conceived without planning

2. Conceived too close to the birth of a previous child

3. A financial strain on the family is created

4. Parents have fear of failure

5. Conflict between parents

6. Thoughts of abortion

7. Wrong sexual preference:

A child may be very much wanted until it is born. The sex prefer-ence is a serious matter with some parents. However, no matter how strong the personal preference might be, it can be very destructive to the child for the parents to reject it because of something for which the child has no control. The sex was predetermined by God and should be accepted by the parents.

Many parents are deeply disappointed over the sex of their children. The rejection of the child may not be done purposely, but done, neverthe-less, with no understanding of the short and long term consequences.

When this emotional wound of rejection occurs, the devil is quick to take advantage of it. Parent rejection due to wrong sex sometimes causes boys to become effeminate, and girls to become masculine. A child who is rejected because it is the wrong sex, will sense it at a very early age. They will often seek to gain parent acceptance by performing as one of the opposite sex.

Consequently, a child who is rejected because of its wrong sex may grow to hate and reject itself. Rejection of one's own sexuality can lead to an open door into many different sexual experiences and life styles.

8. Physical defects

A child born with defects could feel the pains of rejection.

9. Victim of circumstances

Emotional wounds may occur for many reasons and can start at a very early age. Here are some examples of those victims of circum-stance emotional wounds.

A. Rejection may come to a child if the child is left with others while the mother works outside the home.

B. The father may work long hours away from home and may not be able have quality time with his child.

C. Any time the parents devote too little time to their child, the child will usually sense their absence as rejection.

D. Some children are given up for adoption. For the child, this may translate to abandonment by the parents. If so, this produces a severe wound. Although adopted children may be well loved by the adopting parents, many are unable to receive love or to return love properly, because the emotional wound of rejection has already occurred.

E. The death of one or both parents creates a deep wound in the personality of the young child. The child or the adult cannot understand why this has happened to them or their parents. We relate their disappearance as a form of abandonment.

F. Divorce is one of the most disruptive forces in the life of anyone who has experienced it. The wound cuts even deeper when there is strife and conflict in the home.

G. Jealousy in the home environment is also a powerful force. An older sibling in a growing family is often forced to compete with younger brother or sister for parental attention. The new family member may be looked on with jealousy. To a young mind, seeing someone else in mother or father's lap may indicate they love baby instead of me.

10. Victim of abuse

A. Verbal abuse

Some seldom hear a kind or encouraging word. Instead they are degraded, talked down to, and at times, teased. Typical put-downs that give deep emotional wounds in our memory are: "I wish you had never been born;" "You can't do anything right;" "You will never amount to anything;" "You're stupid; " "I wish you were dead," and like comments.

It is very difficult to truly measure the injury that occurs to us when we have experienced this type of verbal abuse.

B. Physical abuse

The physically abused person is immediately filled with fear and confusion, knowing for sure we have been rejected when this happens. Deep down, feelings of hurt and sometimes anger, and the desire to get even and to pay back, begin to build. If this started as a child, many times that person will become an abuser themselves.

C. Sexual abuse

The person who has been subjected to molestation develops an inability to be open and warm with people. We usually display a victim mentality, and lack the ability to trust anyone, especially authority figures. Because we have been "used" in an unnatural way, we feel many deep emotional wounds.

Questions

1. Why does rejection produce such a great amount of negative emotions?

2. Were you rejected in any of these ways you read about?

(Yes__ or No__)

3. If we feel we were rejected at an early age, what can we do about it?

4. In what ways can you relate your past, present, life controlling behaviors to this lesson?

5.   Which of these emotional wounds that you just read about do you feel have had the most impact on your current life?

session five

DEALING WITH LOSSES IN LIFE

One of the most important things we need to learn is how to grieve. Grieving is the ability to recognize deep sorrow and regret over losses we have experienced. God has given us the ability to grieve. If any of us have lost a family member through death, we may or may not have properly grieved that loss.

Problems arise within us when we experience loss in our lives, but we do not grieve those losses. Instead of grieving, we allow ourselves to become hardened inside. As a result, we react to these undealt with emotions in wrong ways, and many of us turn to life controlling behaviors. We can become resentful and angry about our losses and replay them over and over again in our mind. We do not recognize the hurt, pain and loss when we turn to these life controlling behaviors, and we do not allow the Lord to minister to us in those areas.

Some of us have been raised and taught that we are not to cry. Some say real women and men don't cry; therefore brave little girls and boys don't cry, if they want to become real women and men. Real women and men should not show hurt, emotion, or pain. But this is a lie that many have grown up to believe, and some of us have taught our own kids this lie.

We need to see, from a Biblical standpoint, what grieving really is and how Jesus Christ, our model, handled grief. "As soon as Jesus heard the news, (that John the Baptist was dead), He left in a boat to a remote area to be alone…" (Matthew 14:13 NLT, parenthesis, mine.)

Jesus went to a place where He could be alone to grieve for John who had been beheaded by Herod the king.

> "When Jesus therefore saw her (Martha) weeping, and the Jews who came with her, also weeping, He was deeply moved in spirit, and troubled. 'Where have you laid him (Lazarus)?' he asked. 'Come and see, Lord,' they replied. Jesus wept. Then the Jews said, "See how He loved him."' (John 11:33-36 NIV, parenthesis, mine)

Jesus wept at the tomb of his friend, Lazarus, for He was grieved in His spirit.

It becomes a major problem with us when we don't allow ourselves to express the sorrow we feel. We don't realize that if we will be open and honest with God, He will heal us in those areas of our lives. As we bring these things to the light of Christ, He is able to minister His healing to us.

Many of the things that hurt us in our lives have been jammed into the inner recesses or our Soul (mind, will, and emotions) with the hope that they will be forgotten. What we don't realize is that these things continue to affect us in our reactions to the events and the people we encounter daily. We need to learn how to be honest, how to bring these emotions to the surface, and how to grieve about them. As we allow them to surface, God begins a process in us that gives us insight and wisdom about them. This opens the door that allows healing to then take place.

One obstacle to our healing is that when we are hurt, we are able to see only our side of the situation. We are unable to see the situation from God's side. This means we are unable to see the whole picture; we only see one side of it when we have, "one way thinking" controlling us.

When we grieve, we usually need someone to come along side and help us. It isn't necessary for that person to tell us whether we are right or wrong, or to set boundaries for us. They only need to listen and encourage us to share what's really going on deep down with each undealt with emotion.

There is one danger in walking through the emotion of grieving our losses. We can become caught up in it and never allow ourselves to get out. If we are caught up in grieving, we can become very depressed. We can find ourselves filled with self-pity and self-condemnation.

There are generally six stages of grief which usually manifest themselves in the following order.

1. *Denial*: We simply do not want to accept the misfortune of the loss.

2. *Bargaining with God*: God, if you will restore, replace, or repair what we are grieving about, we will do whatever You want.

3. *Anger*: We feel we are totally undeserving of what has happened and feel we have been treated unfairly. This justifies our anger.

4. *Acceptance*: We accept that it happened and we feel we can do nothing about it.

5. *Grief over the loss*: We become honest about our feelings, share those feelings with God and others and allow ourselves to be healed.

6. *Resolution*: We reconcile the relationships we can and resolve to pick up the left over pieces and get on with life.

If we share our thoughts and emotions in each of these stages with the Lord, and receive the input He offers us, we will move through each phase of healing. We will then be able to lay aside our losses and move on to wholeness and healing. If we should get stuck at any point, it is important that we reach out to another believer to help us through.

The most effective way in which to grieve is to grieve one loss at a time. Many of us have a tendency to look into our past and see all the hurt, pain, and abuse, and say, "I can't handle all that, Lord!" It would be like having all our outfits we were going to wear for the entire week, lined up on a table. It would be overwhelming to think we had to wear all the outfits the same day. The fact is we will wear one outfit for each day. And that is the way we should grieve, one loss at a time.

The proper way to grieve is to let the Lord show us which incidents He wants us to deal with, and the order in which He wants us to handle them. It becomes a process, so we don't have the overwhelming sensation that we could never get through it. In the grieving process, we want to be honest about how each incident affected us and the hurt and pain each has caused us.

We also must truly be honest about our sinful reactions to these incidents. These are principles, like judgments and unforgiveness that many of us have violated in our reaction to what we have done to others and what others have done to us. We will discuss some of these in the next session.

Grieving losses are very important and a must if we want true wholeness and healing.

Questions

1. Why is it important for us to learn how to grieve?

2. What happens to us when we do not grieve about our hurts, pains and losses?

3. In what ways do our undealt with emotions affect our relationship with others in our daily walk?

4. Why is it important for us to be able to see both sides of a painful situation?

5. Why is it important for us not to continue too long in our grieving?

6. What is the proper way in which to involve the Lord in our grieving?

7. Share one or more things that you have never properly grieved.

session six

FORGIVENESS

Let's see what Jesus said about forgiveness. "Then Peter came to Him and said, 'Lord, how many times do I forgive a brother or sister who hurts me? Seven?' Jesus replied, 'Seven! Hardly. Try seventy times seven.' The kingdom of God is like a king who decided to settle his accounts with his servant. As he got under way, one servant was brought before him who owed a debt of a hundred thousand dollars.

He couldn't pay up, so the king ordered the man, along with his wife, children, and goods, to be auctioned off at the slave market. The servant threw himself at the king's feet and begged, 'Give me a chance and I'll pay it all back.' Touched by his plea, the king let him off, erasing the entire debt.

The servant was no sooner out of the room when he came upon one of his fellow servants who owed him ten dollars. He seized him by the throat and demanded, 'Pay up, now!' The servant threw himself down and begged, 'Give me a chance and I'll pay it back.' But he wouldn't do it. He had him arrested and put in jail until the debt was paid.

When the other servants saw this going on, they were outraged and brought a detailed report to the king. The king summoned the man and said, 'You evil servant! I forgave your entire debt when you begged for mercy. Shouldn't you be compelled to be merciful to your fellow servant who asked for mercy?'

And his king, moved with anger handed him over to the tortures until he should repay all that was owed him.

> So shall my heavenly Father also do to you, if each of you does not forgive his brother or sister from your heart." (Matthew 18:21-35, paraphrased)

We see from this Scripture, spoken by Jesus Christ our Lord, that forgiveness is a serious matter. Throughout the Bible we find God's "prescription" for us when we are offended. We find that when we refuse to forgive, we suffer as a direct result. Our lives are severely damaged when there is unforgiveness in our heart, and it at times can be torturous to our Souls (mind, will, and emotions).

To forgive is to "release from judgment," and to "give up the right to get even." When we are not willing to release others from our judgment and give up the right to get even, we place ourselves in the position of the man in the story above who was unwilling to cancel the debt of his fellow servant.

His judgment upon his fellow servant was in his own mind. He had the power to decide to cancel the debt and release the judgment. He had the power to decide to throw his fellow servant into jail, and "get even." The decision he made set into force the judgment that came back on him. If we are unwilling to forgive, we will not progress in wholeness and healing, and we will not experience true emotional healing.

The problem is that most of us have been unwilling to forgive, or we didn't know it was necessary to forgive, or we may not have been aware that we held unforgiveness in our hearts. But it is very clear in the Scriptures that forgiveness is a key relational issue in healing and dealing with sins done to us and sins we have done to others. The Bible specifically states, "Therefore confess your sins to one another and pray for one another, so that you may be healed." (James 5:16a)

God gives us this great prescription to get healing and wholeness. Confession and forgiveness will bring healing into our lives. It is the spiritual ointment God uses to soothe our emotional wounds. Confession removes the sting from the wound and forgiveness allows a healing to take place; and in many instances it will restore relationships that have been broken.

Forgiveness has nothing to do with feelings. It is entirely dependent on our will. If we wait until we "feel" like forgiving, we will never forgive. The decision to forgive is made with our will, and as we submit our emotions to God. He will change our will to forgive in due time.

Forgiveness has no bearing on the consequences we experience because of our previous sins. Some people believe if God forgives us for our sins, we won't face any consequences for what we have done. That isn't true. God's forgiveness of our sins and the consequences of our sins are two different things.

For example, let's say you are on the roof of a building, and you look down and say to yourself, "It looks like the ground is about thirty feet down. I believe if I jump down I will make it all right." So you jump, and break both legs. You then realize what you did, made no sense. You pray, "Lord, I ask you to forgive me for my poor judgment. You gave me better sense than that." God will always forgive you for anything, but you still have two broken legs.

The forgiveness of God has nothing to do with the consequences we have established for ourselves. We will always face consequences because they are a direct result of something we have caused to happen. But those consequences have nothing to do with God's forgiveness.

One of the reasons many of us don't forgive could be that we don't understand what forgiveness is. We have some incorrect concepts about forgiveness. Some of us think we have forgiven but we have not. Let's take a closer look at what forgiveness is and is not.

Forgiveness is Not:

1. Overlooking the wrong done to us.

We like to believe that if we overlook a wrong done to us, it has gone away or it will go away. In reality, it never goes away. Our Soul (mind, will, and emotions) is like a computer hard drive that stores things in different boxes that you can bring up at any time. Overlooking something is not forgiveness; it is a form of repression, meaning you just repress the offense and stuff it into your emotional boxes.

Some of us were hurt by what people said or did to us, and we tried to overlook those things. But the truth is, they have had and continue to have a great effect on our lives. Repressing and overlooking offenses we've done to others and those others have done to us does not mean we have forgiven ourselves or them. If there is still pain inside, it is a sign that there is probably unforgiveness still inside.

2. Excusing the wrong done to us.

When we try to make excuses or water down an offense, we are actually trying to tell ourselves that it really wasn't as bad as it seemed. This is justifying, rationalizing, and minimizing, but it is not forgiveness.

3. Analyzing a person's character to explain why the wrong was done.

It is important that we understand exactly what happened, but understanding and forgiveness are two different things. While Jesus was hanging on the cross, He said, "Forgive them for they know not what they do." As we come out of our life controlling behaviors and have some time of sobriety, we may be able to analyze our actions, but we really can't explain them away. (Luke 23:34)

Knowing what has motivated us or others to behave in these ways will help us with forgiveness, but knowing is not the same as forgiveness. We can know about ourselves or another person, and can even know why they behaved the way they did, but still not forgive them or ourselves. Understanding a person's behavior doesn't mean we have forgiven.

Sin is unexplainable. Paul even said in Romans chapter 7 that the things I do, I do not understand.

So we must know that we don't base our forgiveness on our understanding. That means we don't have to understand in order to forgive.

Today many of us and others have spent years in counseling and therapy groups, trying to analyze our lives and understand why we mistreated others and why others mistreated us. We are all too often no better off after these efforts than before we started. Forgiveness is the key that unlocks us from the binding judgments that have caused us so much pain.

It's not always the pain itself that causes us so many problems; it's the lies we believe about the pain that leads us to many life controlling problems. We have to look at ourselves before we can experience healing. It is possible for us to say, "I understand why I did this to someone or why they did this to me. I understand and can see why they may have done this to me, but I just can't forgive them."

If we are unwilling to get beyond our feelings and make a decision to forgive, we will never be able to receive God's healing in our lives. We may finally understand the reason for a person's behavior, but if we don't have the will to forgive, there will be no forgiveness for anyone involved.

4. *Blaming ourselves.*

This happens often in abuse. Taking the blame is not the same as forgiveness. It is proper for us to take the blame for our reaction to these experiences, but being physically, mentally, verbally or sexually abused was not our fault. If we take the blame for it, that is not forgiveness.

Many of us who have been sexually abused have blamed ourselves.

Some may have told us that it was our fault because we played a part in it. If we are convinced it was our fault and take the blame, that is still not the same as forgiveness. It may create the feeling of forgiveness toward the abuser, but that is only because the hurt and pain has been turned inward.

All the above reactions are improper attitudes, which reflect the true state of your emotions, internal problems and misunderstandings. We short-circuit what God wants to accomplish in us if we attempt to substitute any of these attitudes for forgiveness.

What True Forgiveness is:

1. *Facing the wrong we've done to others and the wrong done to us.*

We can neither excuse it nor rationalize it. We have to be honest. Listed below are emotions we feel. Take each emotion by itself, close your eyes and picture in your mind specific events related to them.

A. *Rejection*: Picture events in which you may have felt the need for love and acceptance, but it was withheld from you; you wanted attention, but were ignored.

B. *Neglect*: What you truly needed was overlooked or ignored. A typical example of neglect is when those in the family are out partying and spending all the money on drugs and alcohol, instead of meeting your needs.

C. *Injustice or Unfairness*: This is when the punishment doesn't fit the act done to receive it.

D. *Cruelty or Brutality*: This could have been either physical or verbal. You may have been picked on, called names, or beaten up, or you may have done these types of actions to others. You may have been told you were stupid or that you were never going to amount to anything.

E. *Betrayal*: Adultery is an example of betrayal in a family. Adultery is a betrayal of the love and trust of one for another. The hurt, anger, and pain of betrayal is felt not only by the spouse who has been betrayed, but by the children in the family.

F. *Abandonment*: When a person is abandoned by a loved one or a spouse, the trauma produces deep roots of painful rejection. When a loved one leaves home without a good reason, the abandoned spouse and children suffer greatly. Broken homes register as abandonment in the minds of those it happens to.

Were you able to relate to any of the above events? This is an important exercise, because the first thing we have to do is face the specific wrongs that we have done to others and what others have done to us. We must deal with them specifically, not in generalities. The Holy Spirit works in specifics.

Another title for the Holy Spirit is Comforter and Spirit of Truth. It is the truth about these incidents that will set us free, and His comfort that will allow us to move into wholeness and healing. It is very important for us to face truth in those areas of our lives in which we have hurt and others have hurt us.

2. *Facing the pain, hurt, anger, etc.; not dismissing it with some cliché or saying.*

We don't dismiss hurts and wounds with some all-purpose Christian saying. We can quote a lot of victorious sounding Scripture, but that doesn't get rid of anything. We must bring each incident, one-by-one, and lay them at the feet of Jesus. It states in the Bible that we are to "Give all you worries and cares to God, for he cares about you." (1 Peter 5:7 NLT)

3. Facing and taking ownership for how we reacted to the wrong done to us.

1John 3:15 and Matthew 5:21-26 state that our reaction to our perceived mistreatment may have caused us to treat others the same way we were treated. We may have been filled with anger, hurt and hatred. We may have even committed murder, and if not actually, in our hearts. Our intense reactions have led us far from God. It is important for us to take an honest look at our reactions, how God feels about them, and what we should do about them.

Bring it All to the Cross of Christ.

The cross of Christ is the point at which forgiveness became possible. No human being has the ability to forgive another human being except through what happened at cross. We cannot forgive without God's help, and without our understanding of what took place at the cross. Know this; that God has called us to forgive in Christ. "And be kind to one another, tender-hearted, forgiving each other, just as God in Christ also has forgiven you." (Ephesians 4:32)

The choice is still ours. We don't have to forgive anybody; God has not forced you in the past to forgive and He will not force you now. Even though He has commanded us to forgive, forgiveness is still our free choice. Don't forget the Scripture that tell us if you don't forgive others He will not forgive you.

> "If we confess our sins, He is faithful and just to forgive us our
> sins to cleanse us from all unrighteousness." (1 John 1:9)

Many of us have a problem accepting God's forgiveness. We don't feel as if God can forgive us because we know we don't deserve to be forgiven.

When we understand what happened at the cross, and we see by this Scripture that God wants to forgive us, we begin to understand why God does forgive us. He is a loving God, but He is also a just God, and until Jesus' death occurred on the cross, He couldn't forgive us.

First Thought Wrong

We think, we feel, and then we act. Our first emotional feelings are seldom correct; we call these, "first thought wrong." Here is an example of how that works.

1.) Something negative or hurtful is brought to mind. 2.) We react with first thought wrong: anger, hatred, or resentment. 3.) We make a decision based on our negative feelings. Many of us use life controlling behaviors like food, sex, drugs, alcohol and many more like these simply because we are hurt; we act based on our feelings.

We don't have to follow this process, and many times a day we can choose not to follow this process. The crisis of the will is to make the proper decision, regardless of how we feel. There are some mornings, when the alarm goes off, that we feel like staying in bed. But we make the decision to get up. We ignore how we feel. After we get up and get going, our feelings change. To do this, we have had to make a decision to go against how we felt.

That is what we are facing where forgiveness is concerned. We have to get past our feelings and stop them from controlling our decisions. We must come to terms with what the Word of God tells us; that we are to forgive. Even though we may be hurt or angry, nowhere in God's Word does it say, "Forgive, if you feel like forgiving."

When it comes to forgiveness, the Lord is not concerned about our emotions. He does not expect us to get our emotions lined up in order to forgive. He simply wants us to submit our will to His will, and to forgive, regardless of how we feel.

Our attitude should be, "Lord, I don't feel like forgiving, but I submit my will to your Word. I am willing to forgive." That is the part of our will that we must submit to God. When we take the attitude that we will no longer move on the basis of how we feel, and that it is our decision to obey God's Word, is when true healing begins to take place.

Our emotions will then begin to line up with our decisions. God will take over and change our feelings. We don't have to work to change our feelings. Our responsibility is to submit our will to the will of God. God will then change our feelings.

The Bible, although written long ago, was written for us today. It is always current. The Bible will relate to our lives if we apply it to our everyday situations. If we need to forgive and we are willing to forgive, God has arranged for that forgiveness to take place.

If we are not willing to forgive, we have not entered into repentance. Forgiveness is an act of repentance. We have been walking away from God, harboring bitterness, envy, and hate in our heart. Repentance means to turn around, to turn from our worldly ways and to turn back to God.

This is where we start. Repentance begins when we say, "Lord, I'm going to be obedient to what you tell me." We make a 180-degree turn around from darkness toward God, with a willingness to walk in His light.

We come to terms with the truth as God states it in His Word that we need to forgive. We make a decision based on that truth, regardless of how we feel. This is the point at which we will begin to be set free. When we see the truth about what God has called us to do we will be free. The Bible says "You are truly my children if you obey my teachings. And you will know the truth, and the truth will set you free." (John 8:32)

Questions

1. Look back at a certain event in your life in which you need to forgive someone. Write the name of this person and the violation committed against you. Bring this to someone you trust and be prepared to participate in a relational exercise of forgiveness.

2. Why does God place such a priority on forgiveness?

3. Why is it so difficult to forgive someone who has hurt us?

4. Why is it important for us to face the pain, plus our reaction to it?

5. What part does the cross play in forgiveness?

6. Why is forgiveness not an emotional thing?

THE BUILDING OF YOUR PAST

It is difficult for us to face the reality of how we feel about ourselves. It is therefore difficult for us to be honest with God about how we feel. God can handle the truth about us. Once we get a handle on how we really feel, we can approach Him with complete honesty. He already knows how we feel, so we can drop our excuses, and ask Him to help us get through our problems.

One way to approach God concerning specific incidents in our lives that have had a negative effect on our Soul (mind, will, and emotions) is to picture a high-rise condo. The condo should have one floor for every year of our age. Let's say for example, we are 40-years old. That means we will have a 40-story condo to picture.

Now, let's say on the 40th floor of our lives we invited or re-invited The Lord Jesus to come live in our condo with us. That is when we received the Lord as Savior. Before that time, there were 40 floors in which we lived according to our own lifestyle without the Lord.

When you gave Jesus full control of your life, He came to live with you on the 40th floor, and there were some messes on that floor. There were some rooms, or areas of your life, which were unclean. The first thing Jesus wants to do is help clean up the 40th floor. Jesus doesn't want you living in that mess, and He does not want to live in it either, but He cannot truly change your life until you deal with your floors of undealt with emotions. In reality, He now has come to live inside you;

to become your roommate and help you clean everything up.

Now that He has come to live with us, together we can keep a clean house. Our problems exist from floors 40, on down. We realize there are some messes on the lower floors, but we don't necessarily want to go down and clean up any of them. Even though we can remember those messes and can still feel the hurts from them, we are now living on the 40th floor with Jesus, so we don't want to go back down and experience those messes again.

The Lord isn't willing to leave those messes the way they are. The stench from the lower floors keeps getting stronger, rising up to the 40th floor. Now that we have invited the Lord to live here, He finally gets through to us that we must get on the elevator and go down to one of those floors. We get on the elevator on the 40th floor, a 40-year old man, together with Jesus. We go down to the 7th floor, to an event that happened when we were seven years old.

As a 40 year old man, we recall an event that happened to a seven year old boy. But this time, the Lord is right alongside the 40 year old man. We may ask Him questions about that event. We may ask Him, "Why did this happen, Lord? What made this happen? This hurt very much."

Let's say our father had come home drunk and slapped us against the wall. The slap didn't hurt very much, but something else hurt inside. It was the rejection, the fear, and the unworthiness that came into our emotions.

We need to let the Lord show us that event from a different perspective. We need to be healed from the feelings of that seven year old boy. As we replay this event again in our minds, we usually begin to feel the emotional pain of the boy that got slapped.

We may ask the Lord, "Lord, where were you when this took place?" He will show us where He was. When we were thrown against the wall, the Lord was the one who picked us up. He was the one who got us through the situation. He was present all the time and He cared for us. He will let us see that it hurt Him as much as it hurt us.

This exercise of bringing up each event to the Lord is not some kind of mind game. This is the way we get in touch with significant events in our lives that have deeply wounded us and the others we have deeply wounded. This is the way the Holy Spirit heals us. As we look at the situation with the Lord on our side, we will probably feel the hurt again. We may begin to cry. But the Lord will be there with us. He was there when we were seven years old and He will be there when we are 40 years old.

When we ask Him why He allowed it to happen, why He allowed a seven-year-old to be slapped by a drunk father, His reply may be that there are a lot of things which happen to us that grieve and hurt Him.

We will be able to visualize Jesus, and see that it really did hurt Jesus. We will see also that He experienced the same things we experienced. He was despised, rejected, slapped and abused. And He will show us that the way to get rid of the hurt and pain is to forgive the person who slapped us.

That is just one event down on the 7th floor. Recalling the first event will be the hardest. We will recall the event just as if it happened today, but there will be a major difference. This time the Lord will be with us. We don't go back through it to relive the hurt or get revenge, but to be healed of the hurt. And the Lord will go with us. We will discover we can ask God questions and get answers, because He cares about us.

Most of us don't like to look at our negative emotions because there is always some pain involved. That seven-year-old is still inside the 40 year old man, and he is still hurting. Deep down inside the undealt with emotions of the seven-year-old is adversely affecting our lives.

The Lord can heal us while we visit the 7th floor. When we leave that floor, we may be able to feel sorry for our father. We won't hate him. We won't be angry with him anymore. There may still be some hurt remaining, but not nearly as much as before you visited the floor the first time.

After we clean up this mess and come back up to the 40th floor, we can rest a while. Then we will be able to go down to other floors and clean up other messes. Other people may have caused some of those messes. But a lot of them are ours, especially those caused by our life controlling behaviors.

When The Lord comes along side of us to those areas, we can ask Him, "Lord, what can I do to clean this mess? What can I do to make this right?"

This is when we find it is not a mind game. God will give us mental images. He will take us back to certain events in our lives. One of the things that can help us in this is to remember how Jesus was with little children. He always invited them to come to Him. He never turned them away. God can put that image in our minds. He can show our little seven-year-old that Jesus was there at the time of our pain with His arms reaching out to us.

This can begin the healing process in us. Our seven-year-old, at the moment of the incident, felt as if there was nobody in the world to turn to. Nobody he could love, or who loved him. That feeling has stayed with him for 33 years. It has put doubts in his mind that are still present 33 years later, because it has never been dealt with. But Jesus will bring healing.

Bringing back to mind our past can be very painful. But beyond the pain is the peace and serenity that only the Holy Spirit gives. Jesus said in the book of John that He would give us peace. Not the peace that the world would give to us, but His peace. That is what makes us whole and healthy.

It is not necessary for us to turn over rocks, looking for things to bring to the surface. God will bring up what He wants us to deal with. God will put His finger on whatever He sees that needs healing at this time.

God puts His finger on one important issue at a time. He will not point out the 7th floor, the 11th floor and 15th floor at one time. He will only point out the 7th floor, and say, "Let's go together and deal with that." After we have cleaned out that mess, there will be a period of rest. We will not have to go immediately to the 11th floor. God never puts on us more than we can handle.

We can't change the events of the past, but God can bring healing to the pain that grew out of those negative events. If we are willing to deal with our part of it, the hurt, anger, fear, hatred, and unforgiveness, God will see to it that healing takes place.

Once we start the cleaning up process, our lives will begin to make a positive change. There may be some messes on every floor of our lives. But now we are learning that every time we make a mess we can clean it up with Jesus.

Once we visit a floor and clean it up, we can leave the mess and never go back into that room again. When the Lord comes to live in us we clean up our messes as we go. We deal with the issues as they come up. We allow Him to lead us and we become in a hurry to quickly clean our messes up.

Let's take a moment to see how Jesus re-creates an event in order to accomplish emotional healing.

"Simon Peter followed along behind, as did another of the disciples who was acquainted with the High Priest. So that other disciple was permitted into the courtyard along with Jesus, while Peter stood outside the gate. Then the other disciple spoke to the girl watching at the gate, and she let Peter in. The girl asked Peter, 'Aren't you one of Jesus' disciples?'

'No,' he said, 'I am not!'

The police and the household servants were standing around a fire they had made, for it was cold. And Peter stood there with them, warming himself.

Inside, the High Priest began asking Jesus about his followers and what he had been teaching them.

Jesus replied, 'What I teach is widely known, for I have preached regularly in the synagogue and Temple; I have been heard by all the Jewish leaders and teach nothing in private that I have not said in public. Why are you asking me this question? Ask those who heard me. You have some of them here. They know what I said.'

One of the soldiers standing there struck Jesus with his fist. 'Is that the way to answer the High Priest?' he demanded.

'If I lied, prove it,' Jesus replied. 'Should you hit a man for telling the truth?'

Then Anna sent Jesus, bound, to Caiaphas the High Priest.

Meanwhile, as Simon Peter was standing by the fire, he was asked again, 'Aren't you one of his disciples?'

'Of course not,' he replied.

But one of the household slaves of the High Priest—a relative of the man whose ear Peter had cut off—asked, 'Didn't I see you out there in the olive grove with Jesus?' Again Peter denied it. And immediately a rooster crowed." (John 18:15-27 TLB)

That was the story of the denial of Jesus by Peter; now watch closely, as we see Jesus arrange events in a way to accomplish healing in Peter.

"Simon Peter said, 'I'm going fishing.'

'We'll come, too,' they all said. So they went out in the boat, but they caught nothing all night. At dawn Jesus was standing on the beach, but the disciples couldn't see who he was. When they got there, they found breakfast waiting for them—fish cooking over a charcoal fire, and some bread.

After breakfast Jesus asked Simon Peter, 'Simon son of John, do you love me more than these?'

'Yes, Lord,' Peter replied, 'You know I love you.'

'Then feed my lambs,' Jesus told him.

Jesus repeated the question: 'Simon son of John, do you love me?'

'Yes, Lord,' Peter said, 'You know I love you.'

'Then take care of my sheep,' Jesus said.

A third time he asked him, 'Simon son of John, do you love me?'

Peter was hurt that Jesus asked the question a third time. He said, 'Lord, you know everything. You know that I love you.'

Jesus said, 'Then feed my sheep.'" (John 21:3-17 NLT)

Jesus arranged the same circumstances to heal Peter's undealt with damaged emotions. He restructured the same type of conditions: It was early in the morning, there was a charcoal fire, and Jesus required a threefold confession to repair the damaged emotions caused by the threefold denial.

How awesome and loving that Jesus shows us how much he cares about our damaged emotions to the point that He would restructure this for Peter and us so that we can know for sure that we can cast all our hurts and cares on Him for He cares about these things.

Peter like many of us returned to our old life style before Jesus, and that was his old trade of fishing because of his shame and guilt and his feelings of unworthiness. We have a tendency to react in a similar way when we don't deal with our emotions. Many of us return to our life controlling behaviors.

Jesus told Peter to feed His lambs, take care of His sheep, and to feed His sheep. That is restoration; that is healing. Peter's relationship with Jesus was restored.

When we observe that Jesus recreated the event in order to heal Peter, we see the value of returning to the event so Jesus can accomplish our healing. It is very important that we allow the Lord to do with us as He did with Peter. It is important enough that it was written as an example for us so that we can allow the Lord to take us back to our painful events, so that we can receive healing.

In doing this we can be whole to live out God's purpose for our lives. When we have years and years of undealt with emotions then we tend to create life controlling behaviors to deal with these.

Some of us walk around in constant pain, hurt and anger. God wants to heal it all. The only way for us to be healed of our past hurts is to let the Lord do this for us. No medication, drug, alcohol, sex, or anything we can think of can accomplish this type of healing.

The memory of each incident will stay with us the rest of our lives, but we will no longer feel the damage of it. We will not be angry, or fearful, nor will we feel rejected. Each wound will be healed as we bring them before the Lord.

Because we will get healing in certain areas or our lives, we will be able to reach out and help other people who have personal hurts in those same areas.

Homework:

Pray and ask God to reveal your past damaged emotions and the emotions of others that you may have damaged. On a big poster board, draw your condo and prepare yourself to allow the Lord to take you to each year of your life and show you what you need to clean up. Draw a condo with as many floors as your age. Pray to the Lord on each floor and ask God to reveal to you anything that you did to others or that they did to you that caused a damaged emotion. Write down each incident next to that floor. You may remember things later that you will want to add to each floor. When you get it all done you will start at the 1st floor with a counselor or a friend and visit each damaged emotion. You are to talk fully about how it made you feel as you bring it before the Lord and allow Him to reveal to you how He sees it and how He wants you to view the one you hurt and the one whom hurt you. Then at last, you are to forgive and ask for forgivingness. Ask Jesus to heal you of this hurt. In that back of this book are many prewritten prayers that can help you with this.

Questions

1.   Why is it important for us to know how we really feel about our-selves?

2.   Why is it important for us to have one floor in our condo for every year of our lives?

3.   Why is it important for us to handle only one issue at a time?

4.   What is the same about the way Jesus handled Peter's healing and the way He wants to handle our healing?

5.   Why is it important for us to allow Jesus to reveal and select which areas of our lives He wants to heal and the order in which He wants to heal them?

session eight

JUDGMENTS

"Do not judge others, and you will not be judged. For you will be treated as you treat others." The standard you use in judging others is the standard by which you will be judged. (Matthew 7:1-2)

It is the principle of God that for every action, there is an equal and opposite reaction. As we look at the Scripture quoted above, we may receive some insight as to why we experience a lot of emotional distress. If we have been the victim of child abuse, for example, it is a natural response for us to feel bitter about it. What is occurring, however, is that our hatred and resentment toward the one who abused us may be activating a negative influence in our lives. We are judging, and we are reaping the negative harvest that has left us bitter and hurt.

It usually comes as a great surprise to many of us that we discover we have become just like the ones who hurt us. It is very common for an alcoholic to have an alcoholic parent. Likewise, child abusers have often been abused as children themselves.

When we can come into reality like this and see the big picture, we can see that healing can take place because we see what those who hurt us had experienced. When we begin to see what happen to us emotionally during our lifetime, we can begin to understand what happened emotionally to others during their lifetime.

If God reveals to us that we have become just like our parent, only worse, we can say, "Well, now I understand why my parent did some of the things they did. He did them because he couldn't help it. They were an alcoholic, a sick person, just the same as I am." Many nights we went to bed wishing we weren't an alcoholic and wishing we hadn't done some of the things we did. Our parent must have felt the same way.

But perhaps our loved ones or the ones that hurt us didn't have the opportunity to get godly counsel. Perhaps they died in their addiction or abuse because they had no way out. This should allow us to see that God has been gracious enough to us to give us a way out. When we realize this, we should have no problem letting go of our judgments. God, in his great love for us, is giving us an understanding of ourselves, and an understanding of the ones that we've judged.

"Therefore, you are without excuse, every one of you who passes judgment, for in that you judge another, you condemn yourself; for you who judge practice the same things." (Romans 2:1)

In His principle concerning judgment, God reveals that when we live in an ongoing judgmental attitude, we are captured by that emotional attitude and we become what we are judging. What has happened is that we have become focused on the emotional pain rather than upon our Lord Jesus Christ, and whatever you focus on becomes the driving force in your life. That is why we often find that the things we hated most in the ones that hurt us, we find being practiced in our own lives.

"Don't be deceived, God is not mocked; for whatever a man sows, this he will also reap." (Galatians 6:7)

Whatever judgments we sow against another, we will receive from others. Knowing this, we should desire to sow love and mercy wherever we go. Knowing this, we will receive love and mercy in return.

In the matter of healing judgments, we should look at healing the root causes of the problems in our Soul (mind, will, and emotions). If we have a judgment towards ourselves that we will fail, we will find ourselves constantly failing. If we have an expectation of being rejected, we will bring this judgment of rejection upon ourselves.

Whatever is undealt within our soul is created in where our lives are at today. Whatever we project out through our soul to others is received by their soul and sent back to us. For this reason, we must keep our soul rooted and grounded in a one-on-one daily relationship with our Lord or we will store our emotions and they will become undealt with, and as time goes, many of us will turn back to the only thing that ever gave us relief, and that is our life controlling behaviors.

In dealing with our emotions, we must allow God to go deep into the roots of our heart's attitudes, motivations and character traits. He will do this as we meet with Him daily during our quiet time. He will expose our judgments towards others and ourselves, and challenge us to allow Him to heal them with His love.

Homework:

We need to ask The Lord to show us where we have been judgmental so we can ask His forgiveness and to see where and who we need to ask for forgiveness so we can receive His healing. Write down each person He brings to mind, and one and at time, deal with each incident as with the condo floors. There are prayers in the back of this book to help you with this.

Questions

1. Why should we not judge?

2. In what ways have you became like the ones you've judged?

3. Who have you been judging and in what ways have you judged them?

SOULS THAT TIE TO OTHER SOULS

Soul ties are formed when two or more people have become knitted together. Soul ties can be good or evil. God has created soul ties through the bonding of children with parents, husbands with wives, friends with friends, and Christians with Christians. Soul ties approved by God represent the bonding of people together with the bonds of love.

Let's look at what the Bible says about soul ties.

"For this cause a man shall leave his father and mother, and shall cleave to his wife; and the two shall become one flesh." (Ephesians 5:31)

A husband and wife are bonded together by love.

"Consequently they are no longer two, but one flesh. What therefore God has joined together let no man separate." (Matthew 19:6)

The Bible states that God joins a husband and wife together in marriage, and that is why broken marriages separate the soul tie which God created. That is one reason there is so much pain, sorrow, and trauma in divorce.

The Bible gives us a great example of a friendship soul tie.

> "Now it came about when he had finished speaking to Saul that the soul of Jonathan was knitted to the soul of David, and Jonathan loves him as himself." (1 Samuel 18:1)

> "A man of many friends comes to ruin, but there is a friend who sticks closer than a brother." (Proverbs 18:24)

These both are special kinds of loyalty that exists between devoted friends.

Parent soul ties are in the Bible as well.

> "Now, therefore when I come to your servant my father and the lad is not with us, since his life is bound up in the lad's life (his soul knitted with the lad's soul), it will come about when he sees that the lad is not with us, that he will die…" (Genesis 44:30-31)

When a child is born, the infant should be bonded to its parents. A healthy soul tie should be formed which ministers love and security to that child throughout life. This soul tie serves to stabilize the child's character and personality.

> Christian soul ties are as if, "…from the whole body, being fitted and held together by every joint supplies, according

to the proper working of each individual part, causes the growth of the body for the building up of itself in love." (Ephesians 4:16)

The relationship between Christians is compared to the relationship between various parts of the human body. These soul ties enable the body of Christ to mature and fulfill its calling, proving that we were not meant to live life alone.

Demonic soul ties are formed out of lusts and perversions of the good soul ties that are founded on love and ordained by God.

"Or do you not know that one who joins himself to a harlot is one body with her. For He says, the two will become one flesh," (1Corinthians 6:16)

For example, sexual relationships outside of marriage create demonic soul ties. Through lust, an evil soul tie is formed. This destroys the holy union that was based on love and trust.

And to prove this we will use an example that is very true to men. Every woman that we have ever been with is tied to our soul. How can we prove this? Many times when we are with someone sexually and we are really not into it, we can bring up a memory of someone we were with that we enjoyed and use that person to help satisfy us. We know this is to be true because we have all done it many times. These need to be removed.

Until we get healing and release every demonic soul tie unto the Lord and learn not to pick up new ones, we will continue to create these soul ties. We do it with looks of lust and undressing others with our eyes, television, pornography, magazines, etc. Most of us have ten to fifty soul ties at a time that we can bring up in our mind to satisfy us and sometimes use more than one at a time.

I know this is deep and something most of us have never talked about or thought about. The new saying is, "We have to free up our sexual spank bank," and stop adding to it so that we can fully love our wives and husbands the way God meant for us to love.

If we want a truly great marriage doing this is a must and if you're married now it will bring your marriage to a higher level.

Perverse soul ties are also formed between persons of the same sex. Male with male and female with female are sometimes motivated by things like this, turning our backs on God because of lust, hurt, abuse, and sexual abuse.

This part in the Bible explains it greatly.

"Who changed the truth of God into a lie, and worshipped and served the creature (satan) more than God the Creator, Who is blessed forever. Amen. For this cause God gave them over to degrading passions; for even their women did change the natural use into that which is against nature itself: And likewise also men, leaving the natural use of woman, burned in their lust toward another; men with men working that which is unseemly, and receive in themselves the due penalty of their error." (Romans 1:25-27)

This is a heavy duty Scripture out of the Bible that many never knew existed. Also, perverse soul ties extend themselves to family members, and even animals. This is a very deep subject that needs to be addressed. We will have a tough time being a container that the Holy Spirit dwells in when we have all these things in our soul.

The soul tie between a parent and a child is healthy and beneficial, except when it continues into the adult life of the child. When the son or daughter is ready for marriage, the soul tie with the parents must be terminated in order for a soul tie of marriage to be formed.

When a father gives his daughter in marriage, he severs the soul tie with her, releasing her to her husband. When the soul tie is not severed between the parent and child at that proper time, that which was good and beneficial becomes evil through control and possessiveness.

Sexual perverseness within family relations occurs when there is incest between father/daughter, mother/son, father-in-law/daughter-in-law, brother/sister, brother/brother, etc.

Some of us did not have healthy soul ties with our parents. This left many of us with a sense of incompleteness. This leaves us restless and searching throughout our lives. The enemy can easily draw us into false and perverse soul ties with others.

We also have to look at those we are tied to that died. When a family member or close friend dies, the soul tie formed with that person must be dissolved. The period of sorrow following the death of a loved one is normal. Prolonged mourning indicates the continuation of the soul tie that needs to be broken.

So if we want to be all we can be for Christ we have a healthy soul in which to allow God to do His work in us. God has a great plan for all of us. Although we may feel overwhelmed by all this healing that needs to be done, when we get on the other side of it, it will be wonderful.

Breaking Demonic Soul Ties

The first thing to do is to ask God in prayer to reveal to you any and all soul ties that need to be broken. As He reveals them to you write them down on a piece of paper. A good idea is to go back to session 7 and look at your condo and visit every year of your life and see if there are soul ties to be broken.

When doing this it will be good to find another brother or sister in Christ to do this with. Bring each soul tie before the Lord, one by one. Confess to God that we have gone against His ordinances. Confess that lust has taken us beyond the boundaries of purity that the Lord set for us.

Even if the sin was committed in ignorance, we have found that asking God to forgive each perverse soul tie we have created will bring the most healing. Confessing each out loud, releases it from your soul and we are doing what the Bible says to, "Confess your faults one to another and pray for each other so that you may be healed." (James 5:16)

Confess before God that satan has no further legal right to you. Declare each demonic soul tie that you have identified to be broken in the name of Jesus Christ. Then command the evil spirits associated with the soul ties to leave you in the name of Jesus Christ, the Son of God and never come back.

NOTE: Be as specific as possible when breaking soul ties. Soul ties are formed with each person, television, book, pornography, or animal with whom you have had sexual thought or relation outside of your husband or wife (marriage). Name each person or thing by name or something you associate them with.

Are there any soul ties with animals, family members, perversion, occult, fortune telling, hypnotism, ESP, blood brother or sister covenants, unholy vows, horoscopes, etc.?

There are prayers in back of this book that will help you with this.

Questions

1. In what ways are good soul ties established?

2. In what ways are evil soul ties established?

3. When the proper parent/child soul tie isn't established, what happens?

4. How can family soul ties become perverted?

5. Why do we need to break soul ties?

6. Write down the first 5 soul ties you feel you need to break.

DOES GOD REALLY UNDERSTAND WHAT WE ARE GOING THROUGH

"For I was born a sinner—yes, from the moment my mother conceived me." (Psalm 51:5)

There was nothing any of us we did personally wrong to be born this way. Just like we inherit certain things from our parents when we are born, is the same way we inherited sin into our lives.

> "When Adam sinned, sin entered the world. Adam's sin brought death (to our souls), so death spread to everyone, for everyone sins." (Romans 5:12)

When we look at this through our natural eyes we may feel this is highly unfair. How can God show Himself to be fair and just when He allowed us to be born into this condition through no choice of our own?

> We can see through the Bible that Job felt this way about what happened to him. "For He (God) is not a man as I am that I may answer Him, that we may go to court together, if there was only a mediator between us, who could bring us together." (Job 9:32-33)

Job wanted a face-to-face encounter with God, so God could explain what happened to him. What Job was really saying to God was "God, it would be different if you were a man like me, then you would understand." Our problem is there is no go-between who can bring us together. This was actually the truth in Job's day, but the situation has since changed.

According to the Scriptures, we were born sinners. Because of that, we were also born, in many respects, with the fact that our lives were destined to failure. That is the raw reality. If we were born with that kind of sin nature and that kind of separation from God, it seems that we have been set up to fail, doesn't it?

At first, this appears to put God on the spot. But if we listen carefully to the Bible we are going to have to let God off the hook and put ourselves on the spot instead.

"Therefore the Lord Himself will give you a sign: Behold, a virgin will be with child and bear a son, and she will call His name Immanuel (which means God with us)." (Isaiah 7:14)

Until this prophecy was fulfilled, man and satan could shout all kinds of accusations toward God. "God, you're unfair," "God, you don't understand," "God, you're not a man."

About 800 years before Jesus was born, God revealed His forthcoming birth through prophets writing prophecy that came true. Until this event, man and the devil felt they had a legitimate argument with God, but when this prophecy became a reality it changed the relationship between God and man.

At this point, God united Himself with us. He became flesh; He took on our humanity, and identified Himself with us. Now, He wants us to learn to identify ourselves with Him. If we can come to understand this, we will have accepted a mighty revelation.

God came down to this earth and began to experience life from our perspective. The God of the universe, in the Person of His Son Jesus, came through the vessel of the Virgin Mary. He entered our world, experienced our temptations, hurts, rejections, pain, and loneliness, etc. He opened Himself to be attacked by the same sinfulness that attacks us. That is what God did through Jesus.

Because of that, we now have a mediator, an umpire. We can no longer use the excuse that God doesn't understand. We can't get away with that. God did this to bring healing, deliverance, and salvation to His people. He brought to us the fullness of who He really is. As a result, we can now enter into the fullness of God.

But it is hard for us to let any part of God come into us when we are so full of ourselves. Our emotions are filled with what we have done to others and what others have done to us since we took our first breath. Our lives have been stuffed with sinfulness, hurt, rejection, woundedness and junk. It becomes obvious that when we ask Jesus to come into our lives, there isn't much room left for Him.

Thankfully Jesus takes us just as we are. He takes the smallest part we give Him, and begins the process of identifying His presence within us. We need to allow this. It is not enough for us to understand that we have been rejected during our lives and have caused rejection in others. It is not enough for us to understand we have damaged emotions. It is not enough to simply understand that we are wounded people.

Understanding our problem is only the start. Unfortunately, many of us, once we get an understanding of why things are like they are, go back to life controlling behaviors and back to being wounded and sick, because we now have an understanding of why we are the way we are. That gives us a reason to continue being that way.

Emotional sickness is "in" right now and is big money in the world. It is "in" to have something emotionally wrong with you. People spend millions going to psychiatrists and doctors and health clinics, so some-one can tell them there is something wrong with them. People say, "I'm a child of an alcoholic, I have ADD, I have depression, I have PTSD, and I now understand why I behave the way I do."

But as we allow the Bible to identify with us through others and Jesus, we will see health and wholeness begin to enter our lives. The Apostle Paul actually came to a level of maturity where he could rejoice in his infirmities, because God could manifest His strength in Paul's weaknesses.

We need to see the depth of what God actually accomplished. He not only identified Himself with our flesh, He also identified with our human life situations. He even aligned Himself with a dysfunctional family background.

Matthew chapter one contains the family tree of Jesus. Perhaps there are some strange people in your family tree. Sometimes, we use that for an excuse: "I'm overweight because there are four generations of overweight people in my family."

Let's take a look at the family tree of Jesus. First of all, Jesus was called the son of David. David was the greatest king Israel ever had, in the flesh. But as David got comfortable and relaxed in his laurels, he also got lax in his walk with God. He committed adultery and murder, yet he is in the family tree of Jesus.

Also, there was Abraham. Abraham had a terrible problem with fear and with lying. God told him to go in a certain direction, but be-cause there was a famine in the land he went to Egypt, instead.

He feared the king, because Abraham had a beautiful wife and he thought the king might kill him and take her for himself. So he told Sarah to tell the king she was his sister, which she did. When the king took her in, God caused havoc in his house, and the king confronted Abraham for lying. Later, Abraham did the very same thing. He re-lapsed.

God had promised Abraham a son, and he wanted to see the promises of God fulfilled. He also had a problem with impatience. He wasn't willing to wait on God because God was moving too slowly.

Sarah came up with a plan. She suggested that Abraham should go to her handmaiden, Hagar, and let Hagar conceive. Abraham gladly complied, but God would not accept that son as the promise of the covenant. Abraham was a man just like we are, in that he had problems, yet he is in the family tree of Jesus.

Abraham's grandson, Jacob, was also less than perfect. He was a deceiver, a schemer. He stole the birthright from his older brother, and deceived his father by putting hairy skins on his arms. Even though God had promised to bless him, he still manipulated and deceived.

However, his life drastically changed one night after he wrestled with an angel of the Lord. God changed his name to Israel, which means, "Overcomer; Prince of God." He is also in the family tree of Jesus. Can we appreciate the scope of this? God is not interested in our background.

There was also a woman named Ruth. She wasn't even a Jew, she was a Moabite. She was a Gentile, yet she was in the family tree of Jesus. There are some adulterous women in His family tree, such as Tamar, Rahab the prostitute, and others.

It is important for us to see how He identified with us. His family tree by human standards was just like ours. It was full of sinful human beings. But Jesus did not use that as an excuse. He did not let it affect Him. A lot of us have been blaming others all of our lives because our parents were not what they should have been.

It's time we let our parents off the hook. They were the product of the generation before them. Dysfunction gets passed down through generations. That may be the reason we are the way we are, but it is not a legitimate excuse to stay the way we are.

Jesus took on a family tree like many of ours so He could identify with us and we could identify with Him. He humbled Himself to that depth. What does that say about our God?

He also had an opportunity to experience the same kind of wounds we experience. Matthew's Gospel also reveals something about that. We should admire the parents of Jesus the more we study them. Joseph was a good man, but inadvertently he did something a lot of fathers have done, especially in our generation. During the betrothal period, Joseph and Mary were not allowed to see each other, so they obviously had no physical contact.

When Joseph discovered Mary was pregnant, he decided to divorce her quietly. Now, how did that affect the child in the womb? Psychologists have determined that a child can be affected while in its mother's womb. So we see that Jesus was rejected in the womb by his earthly father. That rejection didn't last long, because an angel visited Joseph and explained that Mary was telling the truth.

There are many cases of children suffering rejection while young. It is not uncommon to have a husband walk out on his wife during her pregnancy. It is not inconceivable to expect the mother to lay awake nights thinking it would be a whole lot easier if she weren't pregnant. That could generate a lot of rejection. A child may be born not knowing its parent or parents, never hearing its parent's voice. It is important to young children for Dad and Mom to be there.

That is the sort of thing we must let Jesus identify with. When Jesus is allowed to enter that type situation, He will take the hurt away. We identify with Jesus, and we allow Him to identify with us. Many of us need to let Jesus identify with us at the point of all the undealt with emotions in our lives.

"And she gave birth to her first-born son; and she wrapped him in cloths, and laid him in a manger, because there was no room for them at the inn." Joseph and Mary were both of the lineages of David. That meant their parents were also of the lineage of David. It is possible that at least one set of parents had a home in Bethlehem, since it was the City of David. Also, being the age they were, it is highly unlikely that both sets of parents were dead. (Luke 2:7)

That raises a question. Why would Joseph and Mary go to an inn, when they probably had at least one set of grandparents living in town? The answer is that their parents rejected them because of the pregnancy issue. So, we see that Jesus was turned away by other members of His family.

In addition, He was turned away from the inn. There was much rejection and other negative emotions in the early experiences of Jesus. Again, we can see that He entered into and identified with many forms of our hurt.

"No one of illegitimate birth shall enter the assembly of the Lord, none of his descendants, even to the tenth generation, shall enter the assembly of the Lord." (Deuteronomy 23:2)

Jesus also experienced generational curses. The strongest curse in the Old Testament is found in that verse.

The illegitimate person was excommunicated from the congregation, and so were his descendants to the 10th generation. This is any child who was born without a father. That gives us an indication of how important fathers are in God's eyes. Like some of us, Jesus had been called illegitimate all His life.

"And so they were saying to Him, 'Where is Your Father?' Jesus answered, 'You know neither Me, nor My Father; if you knew Me, you would know My Father also.' The Pharisees are saying, 'You, who have no father, who are you to tell us about our father? Our father was Abraham.'" But Jesus responded by telling them their father was the "father of lies," the devil. (John 8:19)

"Christ redeemed us from the curse of the law, having become a curse for us—For it is written, 'CURSED IS EVERYONE WHO HANGS ON A TREE'..." (Galatians 3:13)

It was no accident that Christ identified Himself with being illegitimate, of being subject to the strongest curse in the Old Testament. By going to the bottom meant He covered all of the curses.

We may have generational curses in our families, but that means nothing to Jesus because He has identified with all curses. For the born-again believer, He has broken all curses, which may have been passed down through the family. Even if addiction has wrecked our families for three generations, it will not wreck the fourth generation. That won't happen if we let Jesus identify Himself with the curse in us. He will take it upon Himself and remove it from us. He wants to do that with each of us.

"Since then the children share in flesh and blood, He Himself likewise also partook of the same, that through death He might render powerless him who had the power of death, that is, the devil; and might deliver those who through fear of death were subject to slavery all their lives. For assuredly He does not give help to angels, but He gives help to the descendants of Abraham. Therefore, He had to be made like His brothers in all things, that He might become a merciful and faithful high priest in things pertaining to God, to make payment for the sins of the people, for since He Himself was tempted in that which He suffered, He is able to come to the aid of those who are tempted." (Hebrews 2:14-18)

These verses show us Jesus also identified with our temptations. The Bible says He was tempted in all points. We have no reason to remain sick or wounded any longer.

Jesus is able to help us because of what He accomplished. The Bible tells us there is no temptation which is not common to man. When that temptation comes, God will provide a way of escape. James said, "Blessed is the man who endures temptation, for after he has been tested, he will receive the crown of life." If He says we can endure it, we can endure it, because the power of Jesus Christ comes into us to identify with us. (James 1:12)

"Since then we have a great High Priest who has passed through the heavens, Jesus the Son of God, let us hold fast our confession. For we do not have a High Priest who cannot sympathize with our weaknesses, but one who has been tempted in all things as we are, yet without sin. Let us therefore draw near with confidence to the throne of grace that we may receive mercy and may find grace to help in time of need." (Hebrew 4:14-16)

Our High Priest can sympathize with our weakness. He was tempted in all points, yet He was without sin. Jesus walked the earth for 33 years and He never gave in to sin. That tells us about the magnitude of His temptation. Once we give in, it is not difficult for satan to get us to sin again. On the other hand, if someone has never submitted to sin he can expect to receive a double dose from the devil, which is intent upon making us all fall.

The Bible says we are to come boldly before the throne of grace, that we may obtain mercy and find grace to help in the time of need. We usually get that backwards. We run to God for help when we're already in the time of need. But He is telling us to come beforehand so we'll be ready in our time of need.

So we can see Jesus entered the world through a dysfunctional family tree. He identified with us in that respect. He also identified with our brokenness. He took it on and walked through our temptations and weaknesses, and He is now our merciful and faithful High Priest.

When we pray to God about our struggles, He is there to identify with us, to give us grace and mercy and help. He is waiting for us to tell Him, "Jesus, take this; identify with me and help me."

The Bible tells us Jesus was despised and rejected; He was a man of sorrows (pains); He was acquainted with grief (sicknesses); He was wounded for our transgressions; He was bruised for our iniquities; the chastisement of our peace was upon Him, and by His stripes (lashes), we are (have been) healed. (Isaiah 53:3-5)

The Bible says that Jesus is the last Adam. He came to restore and to recover what the first Adam lost. The first thing He encountered as He started His ministry was the wilderness experience with the devil. He faced three temptations in the wilderness. It is interesting that we can find three similar temptations in the Garden of Eden.

The first temptation involved food. For Adam, it was the fruit of the knowledge of good and evil. For Jesus, it was turning stones into bread.

But Jesus said, "Man shall not live by bread alone." (Matthew 4:4)

The second temptation involved the deception of magic. Satan appeared as magical creature that had great wisdom. Satan also tried to tempt Jesus to do something God had not told Him to do, with the promise that if He did, everyone would follow Him.

The third temptation implied that God had lied to Adam and Eve, and if they would eat of the fruit they would be as God. Likewise, the devil promised Jesus the kingdoms if He would simply bow down before him.

We can see that Jesus identified with Adam by experiencing the same type of temptations. But He refused to be deceived by the devil. Jesus lived 33 years of perfection, meeting every temptation and deception through His faith in the Father. He then walked to Calvary and exchanged His life for the life of Adam and all his descendants.

It is good for us to understand that we have experienced hurt, pain, and rejection. Now it is time to allow Jesus to identify with all of these undealt with emotions, and heal the wounds caused by them. Also, it is good for us to understand the inner problem we may have discovered. We can no longer sit around and continue to live in this misery. We are to let Jesus identify with our negative emotions and take them from us.

God may show us that we have experienced all kinds of abuse in our lives, but Jesus can handle it all. Let Him identify with each one. Remember those Roman guards who put their fists in Jesus face? They spit in His face and called Him every horrible name under the sun. He can understand abuse.

The key to emotional healing is to accept the good news of the Gospel: that Jesus Christ came to earth, entered our level—no matter how low— and offered Himself for us freely. He willingly poured out His blood for our redemption. Our healing is involved in taking that truth and applying it to our soul. The key is in the application of the good news to our soul.

When we give things to Jesus, it is really an unfair exchange because we get all the benefits. Jesus tells us, "I know you have been rejected, so I want to take your rejection from you and give you My acceptance. I want to take your sense of unworthiness from you and give you of My worth." (Isaiah 53:3-5)

That is the application of the Gospel at a level where soul healing will really take place. We are not to get caught up in identifying with being rejected, neglected, or terrorized. Those can become excuses for failure. We must begin to allow Jesus to identify Himself with us. We have to let Him give us His identity.

> "I have been crucified with Christ; and it is no longer I who live, but Christ lives in me; and the life which I now live in the flesh I live by faith in the Son of God, who loved me, and delivered Himself up for me." (Galatians 2:20)

That needs to be our daily experience. Whatever our problems happen to be, in our quiet time we need to tell Jesus, "Jesus, I come to you and I identify this part of me, this weakness, this woundedness, this sinfulness. I really need to identify this with You, and I ask you, in place of that, identify with me Your health and strength and the godliness that is You. I want to relate to You from the perspective of who I am in You, not who I am in the flesh."

In exchange, as we willingly give Him those things, He gives us His righteousness, His health, His wholeness and His right standing with God.

> "And when you were dead in your transgressions and the uncircumcision of your flesh, He made you alive together with Him, having forgiven us all our transgressions, hav-

ing canceled out the certificate of debt consisting of decrees against us and which was hostile to us; and He has taken it out of the way, having nailed it to the cross." (Colossians 2:13-14)

When we know in our hearts we have received Jesus Christ as our Savior, this Scripture becomes ours. It is as if we have a bank account with God. He has recorded all we have ever done, both the good and bad, in a book of remembrance, and this is all we have to offer Him on the Day of Judgment. But when we received Jesus as Lord and Savior, God wiped out the handwriting of requirements that was charged against us. We had an incredible debt we could never pay, but when we took Jesus into our heart, God canceled our debt; marking it, "paid in full."

"In Him, you also, after listening to the message of truth, the gospel of your salvation—having also believed, you were sealed in Him with the Holy Spirit of promise, who is given as a pledge of our inheritance, with a view to the redemption of God's own possession, to the praise of His glory." (Ephesians 1:13-14)

By this we can see that He didn't leave the account empty. What He has started in us, He will complete.

If we ever decide to go in the other direction, we will never enjoy things of the world the way we once did. We will not enjoy sin any more. We will not enjoy life controlling behavior like getting high or getting drunk, or having sex outside of God. We will give up those things.

The Holy Spirit came to live in our hearts when we received Jesus Christ as our Savior. He is the guarantee that we will receive the inheritance of God. He is like a down payment on what is to come. God placed in our account with the down payment that guarantees we will receive His inheritance.

Some of us still have a hard time believing that. We have become so accustomed to believing lies all of our lives that the lies seem like the truth in our minds. Now, when the truth comes, the lies in our minds say, "No, that isn't the truth." So, we have to go to war against the lies, and we do it with the truth of the Gospel.

The Scripture says we are sealed. Back in the old days, the kings wore signet rings, which carried a copy of their own face. After they had written a mandate, they would impress their signet ring on the wax seal. The seal conveyed the message that it was the mandate of the king.

God has taken His own impression, His own signet and He has placed His mark upon us. It is His statement to the world that we are His possession. That is why the devil hates us so much. We belong to God, and we carry His mark.

Questions

1.   Write down some areas of your life that come to mind in which you need to let Jesus identify.

2.   In what way did God provide us with a mediator, or an umpire who can under-stand our human feelings?

3.   Why is it important for us to be aware of the family of Jesus?

4.   If we have inherited certain dysfunctional characteristics, which have been passed down to us through previous generations, what should we do?

5.   How do we let Jesus identify with our dysfunction?

6.   Why is it important for us to come to Jesus before our time of need rather than wait until our time of need, and then come to Him?

7.   What is the real key to you getting emotional healing?

session eleven

WHAT SOUL HEALING LOOKS LIKE

"And do not be conformed to this world, but be transformed by the renewing of your mind, that you may prove what the will of God is, that which is good and acceptable and perfect."
(Romans 12:2)

In regards to renewing the mind, we have had many opportunities during these sessions to forgive everyone who has caused us harm during our lifetime. This is a giant step in the process of renewal. Now it is time to see how well we have done in the area of forgiveness.

Perhaps we have been told that unless we are able to forget, we really haven't forgiven. But that is simply untrue.

For example, everyone probably has scars that have healed. We all have scars we can point to. We experienced some sort of physical mishap, which caused an abrasion in our skin. It probably bled for a while, and then it scabbed over. Finally, it healed.

After it healed, it became a scar. Now, as we relive that experience, we can still remember it well, but we do not feel any of it, physically. We can remember it and point to it, but we no longer feel the pain.

Is such a thing possible emotionally as well as physically? Is it possible that we might be able to remember a past hurt, yet not feel the hurt in the present? It is time for us to understand that although we have been hurt inside, and we have suffered because of the emotional things that have happened to us, it isn't necessary for us to forget those things.

Forgetting is not necessarily a part of the healing process. As a matter of fact, Jesus Christ would have us not forget those things. He wants to heal our hurts and let them become scars, which we can point to for His glory. There is nothing wrong in having a scar. A scar can be a plus. We need to get beyond the scars and begin thinking about how Jesus is going to lead us from this point onward. We can look at the incidents in our lives that hurt us and the ones we had done that have caused hurt to others and allow Jesus to heal the hurts, and then use those incidents to His glory by helping others.

It is important for us to discover our purpose in life. It may never have occurred to us that one of the purposes in our lives is to utilize the scars in our lives to His glory. Imagine what it would be like to be able to point to an emotional scar and tell a hurting person, "I know what you are going through, because I have experienced that hurt. That happened to me also."

"But look here, it has healed. I can tell you the details; I can tell you everything that happened, I can remember word for word what took place, but you see, I don't feel the pain anymore, because it is healed. God healed it in me; therefore, He can heal it in you."

Every one of us has at least one incident, and some of us have many incidents in our lives, which have been traumatic to us. We now have a choice while we are receiving the healing ourselves, to use what we are learning to help others in the future as part of our purpose.

Have we really forgiven?

There is one sure way in which we can tell whether or not we have forgiven someone: When we talk about it, when we share it, are we picking at a scab, or are we pointing to a scar? We can pick at the scab, and it will never heal. We can continue to pick at the scab, and continue, and continue, and it will continue to bleed, and continue to hurt, and continue to fester, and continue to poison us.

We may even deliberately pick at it to make it bleed some more. We may even want to feel the pain again. It may have become a way for us to manipulate others, or to receive sympathy from someone.

The alternative is to give the hurt to God and allow Him to heal it. We can let it become a scar so we will be able to point to it, and say, "God healed this. I know what you're going through; I went through the same thing. But God healed it. Let me tell you about it, because He can heal you, too."

It becomes obvious that we have to begin to think beyond where we are this moment. We have to think beyond the suffering we may be feeling right now. We can get ourselves beyond that, because God has another purpose for us.

Do we realize how unique we are? We may not feel very unique, but stop to think a moment. How many people are embroiled in addictions and life controlling issues in the world? Certainly, millions of people are victims of addiction. And many people have been exposed to secular programs where they have been taught why they became addicts.

They came away from those programs able to say, "Okay, now I know why I use," but they continued to use.

That is not the case with us. This is an entirely different type of counseling approach. Those millions of addicts are not exposed to true emotional healing, but we are. That makes us unique. In our counseling, we discover there is a Divine purpose for us being where we are.

When God breathed life into us, He didn't do it because He thought it would be nice and cute for us to be born. He has a Divine purpose for our lives. However, we will not realize that successful walk with God until we get beyond our scabs.

We have to move into a scar status in order to reach the fulfillment of God's plan, because the scabs will stand in the way of God's purpose. The reason is that the scabs will always influence our responses and our reactions to everything that occurs in our lives. So long as our wounds are still bleeding, so long as we are still picking at them, subconsciously they have an effect upon our response to everything that is said to us. Every situation that occurs in our lives will be filtered through our emotional scabs until those scabs have been healed.

Let's think for a moment. What would we look like if we had only scabs and no scars? And suppose every day we would keep knocking or picking those scabs loose. We would be bleeding all over everything. Wouldn't that be a mess?

Now, let's look at it through the eyes of God. Imagine how we look in God's eyes when we refuse to receive His healing power for our emotional hurts. All that internal bleeding, an absolute mess inside, because we insist upon picking at the emotional scabs!

How does God feel about that type of rebellion against His love? There He stands, with outstretched arms, ready to heal us, but we turn our backs on Him. Instead, we go into a corner and pick at our emotional scabs and cry ourselves to sleep. Is that how we want to spend the rest of our lives, as scab pickers, instead of being able to point at scars? The reality is that those of us who refuse to forgive are scab pickers.

So we are faced with a decision. Jesus Christ always works on the basis of our will, not our emotions. He always brings us to a point of choice. Now He has led us to the point of having to make a decision concerning what we are going to do about certain situations in our lives. That decision cannot be based upon our emotions.

He has brought us to that point, right now, concerning the things we have been picking at and allowing to bleed. He is saying to us, "I am ready to make scars out of those wounds, how about you? Are you willing to receive My healing, or would you rather continue to walk around and pick at the scabs?"

If we decide to continue to pick at the scabs, what we are actually saying is, "I'm going to continue on the program I have always been on, centering on myself. I'm going to concentrate upon myself and all the things that have happened to me. I'm going to focus upon that, and have my own pity party. I refuse to allow You to heal me, Jesus." That is a form of rebellion in God's eyes, but He gives us the free choice to do it.

He will always give us the choice. What we need to see clearly is that our decision cannot be based upon our emotions. It is solely our decision to say, "Jesus, I know You can heal; therefore, I'm going to allow You to heal me." We lay the wounds at His feet, and we give Him an opportunity to heal them. After that, we can start thinking in terms of our successful walk with Him.

Most of us who enter counseling/rehab/jail programs are centered upon ourselves. Our idea of success is to become addiction free. Our thought is, "If I can attain being clean and sober in this program and if I can hang onto that, I'll be successful."

That is all right in the beginning, but we really need to begin thinking in the next dimension. There is no sense in attempting to stay drug free, until we get rid of our emotional hurts. We will never attain true success so long as we are still bleeding, emotionally.

We must understand that we are in charge of what we do with our lives. We can release control of our lives to somebody else, but we can't release responsibility for our lives to anybody. Many of us have released control of our lives to other people and to circumstances in which we have found ourselves. But we haven't been able to release responsibility, because that is impossible. The responsibility for our lives still rests with us.

You are no one's victim without your permission. That wasn't true when we were children, but it is true now. We no longer have to be the victims we were as children, unless we give those wounds permission, unless we insist upon picking at the scabs.

One thing for certain, we are never going to have public success until we have private success. We must have healing and wholeness within our lives before we can have success out in life. The only way to overcome the world is to overcome the world in us. And the only way to overcome the world in us is through Jesus Christ, who said, "I have overcome the world!" So, we are constantly brought back to Jesus, who is our High Priest.

> "Therefore, holy brethren, partakers of a heavenly calling, consider Jesus, the Apostle and High Priest of our confession." (Hebrews 3:1)

It is time for us to begin to look to Jesus as our High Priest. It is necessary for us to see Him in this role in order accomplish our healing.

> "Now the main point in what has been said is this: we have such a High Priest, who has taken His seat at the right hand of the throne of the majesty in the heavens, a minister in the sanctuary, and in the true tabernacle, which the Lord pitched, not man. For every High Priest appointed to offer both gifts and sacrifices; hence it is necessary that this High Priest also have something to offer." (Hebrews 8:1-3)

Every High Priest must have something to offer. Obviously, Jesus does not have to keep offering His blood over and over again. Once was enough. So, what does He have to offer now? He has the sacrifices we take to Him. He is standing, as our High Priest, with His hands outstretched, waiting for each of us to come to Him and lay in His hands those things in our lives we are willing to give Him control over.

If we have certain personality characteristics which are not good, we can lay those in His hands. Our High Priest has His all-consuming fire going constantly, day and night, 24 hours a day. And what is most important is that he is also ready to take our scabs from us. He is ready to take them from us and heal them with His all-consuming fire. A wound that is sealed by fire is cauterized. That is, it is sealed by intense heat. He is ready to cauterize our wounds and leave us scars as evidence of our healing.

If we want to step from scab to scar, to healing and success, now is the time. So, let's take a few minutes, right now, to write down those areas inside us that need to be healed. We will ask the Holy Spirit for revelation and trust Him to reveal the wounds within us that are still bleeding. We will ask the Holy Spirit to reveal to us those whom we have never really forgiven.

Even though you have gone through the condo session, this is now the time to deeply look and allow the Holy Spirit to reveal if you have truly forgiven others and most of all, yourself.

It is not that these people deserve to be forgiven. We are forgiving out of obedience to God's command, trusting that He will set us free from the emotional pain. We will ask the Holy Spirit to reveal to us those attitudes and characteristics and thought patterns which are not pleasing to Him. This is our opportunity to have a moment of truth with our Lord.

Take time and write down and record any and everything the Holy Spirit brings to the surface to be healed.

Now, let's visualize Jesus Christ as our High Priest. That doesn't mean we have to see Jesus Christ in our minds. We just need to visualize Him as being our High Priest in the holy of holies in Heaven. He said we could come into the throne room with boldness, so He expects us to do that. He wants us to get beyond the scab, into the scar, and on to success with Him. Our ultimate goal should be to fulfill God's purpose for our lives, regardless of what that might be. That is true success.

EXERCISE:

If possible, divide into groups of two to three persons each. Arrange chairs so they are facing each other.

This is important. Do not pray "for" each other. Instead, one to two of you support the third person as he takes his scabs to the Lord. Simply be beside him as he prays for himself, and lend him your support.

INSTRUCTIONS FOR THE PERSON WHO PRAYS:

Go into the presence of Jesus and confess to Him that you have the scabs you have written down. Then visualize yourself giving those scabs to Jesus. Ask Him to heal those areas of your life; picture Jesus taking those scabs from you. Identify them specifically, whether they are people, or circumstances, or attitudes, etc. Be specific.

You are releasing those specific scabs to Jesus, your High Priest. You are asking Him to heal them, to cauterize them, to seal them with His all-consuming fire. He will take those things from you and let them become scars in your life. You will then be able to point to them as being healed. In this fashion, God will be glorified.

The other two members of the group are to support that one as he is taking his scabs to Jesus. Do not interfere with him, or pray for him, just support him quietly. You are giving him spiritual strength. That is ministry. Repeat this process until everyone in the group has had an opportunity to release his wounds to the Lord.

Remember: Part of the process of having our emotional wounds healed is forgiving the people who have hurt us and doing this daily!

Questions

1. Record what the Lord accomplished while you were in your group or with one person.

2. Why is it unnecessary for us to forget in order to forgive?

3. Why is the act of forgiving a necessary part of healing?

4. Why are scars positive rather than negative?

5. In what way is refusing God's healing a form of rebellion?

6. Why is it important for us to accept Jesus as our High Priest?

7. What does true healing look like for you?

session twelve

MAINTAINING YOUR EMOTIONAL HEALTH AND SETTING GOALS

One of the main things that will come against us to try to get us unhealthy is the lie of low self-esteem and not having any goals.

Low self-esteem is a scab in our lives. Low self-esteem has an effect upon everything that transpires during our lifetime. Every circumstance and every situation that occurs throughout our lives, we filter through our feelings.

Low self-esteem has an initial cause, and it has a maintenance factor. Some causes of low self-esteem can be put-downs, such as:

"You can't be trusted not to return to your life controlling behaviors."

"You're never going to amount to anything!"

"Why are you so stupid?"

A myriad of put-downs by others, who didn't realize what they were doing, have programmed us into having a low opinion of ourselves. We respected the wisdom of others, so we received their put-downs as truth.

These can be some causes of low self-esteem. We continue to believe we are less than worthwhile because we really don't know who we are in Christ.

When we were conceived, when we became form and substance in our mother's womb, the Lord, by His Spirit, gave us a spirit. He breathed life into us. There is no life without God. God is the Author and the Finisher of life.

Man has tried over and over to create life, but he has never been successful. For example, we can manufacture a seed so that it will look and feel exactly like a real seed. We can even plant it, but it will not grow, because it must have God's life in it.

God imparted life to us. We became a spirit person. Now, because we were not supernaturally conceived, we inherited the genetic nature of Adam. We inherited the ability and the nature to sin, right there in the womb. It came genetically, down through mankind, from Adam to our parents.

When we came forth into the world, we had the sin nature in us. But, we were still a spirit person. Our life is in our spirit. When we die our spirit doesn't die, only our flesh dies. Our spirit goes either to be with the Lord, or it goes to Hell.

Then, at the moment we accepted Jesus Christ as our Savior, something supernatural happened. Transplantation took place in us. The old man, the old spirit person, became fused with Christ, and God considered him as crucified, dead and buried with Christ. He then imparted to us a new nature, a new man, and a new spirit person incapable of sin.

Inside us is a spirit being which contains the Spirit of Christ, and the Spirit of Christ is incapable of sin. We have within us this spirit person, this new being, this new birth, which says, "I am incapable of sin, and I will not sin. There is no way in the world I am going to sin."

Now, we have a mild problem in all of this. God couldn't give us a supernatural body without killing us, so He put that new nature, that new spirit being incapable of sin, into our old earthen vessel. And the old earthen vessel was programmed by the old man with the sin nature from Adam. It has developed certain personality characteristics and habit patterns that are sinful.

We are confronted with a battle between the new nature and the old nature habit patterns that remain. They are only leftovers from the influence of the old man, but they are still powerful habits. Inside us we have those natural tendencies, those natural habit patterns with the disposition to sin. But that is all they are, habit patterns established down through the years of programming by our old man.

Our challenge is the necessity to bring out the new nature, the nature incapable of sin, while eradicating the old habit patterns. Most of us try to do this by our own will. We determine, "I will not do that anymore!" Unfortunately, the will is part of our flesh, so we have a situation in which flesh is fighting flesh, and there is not going to be a spiritual victory.

There is a solution, and we can find it right in the Bible. John the Baptist didn't say, "I must decrease, that He may increase." He said, "He must increase, but I must decrease." (John 3:30)

The only way to win the battle which is going on inside is to bring in more of Jesus Christ, to focus upon Jesus Christ. Whatever we focus upon tends to grow larger within us. As we bring in more light by focusing upon Jesus, there is less room for darkness. The main thing upon which we need to concentrate is our Lord and Savior, Jesus Christ. As pastor and author Peter Lord says, "You have to keep the main thing the main thing."

This has very much to do with what kind of music you listen to, what you are watching on TV, what type of things are you talking about, and what type of conversations you are listening to. This is not just a one-time healing process; this is a radical life style change.

We have to look at it as when we are in active addiction. If we did not have what we were addicted to many of us would be sick and miserable and even have thoughts of suicide.

We need to get into a deep relationship with Jesus Christ like we did with our life controlling behaviors. The deeper the relationship with Jesus, the greater His opportunity to make the necessary changes within us. And the more changes that take place in our flesh, the more that old nature is washed out.

At times we will not even be conscious of the change because we are not accomplishing it on our own. But when we look back over time, a few months from now, we can see we have changed. Not because we did it deliberately, it was the effect of concentrating upon Jesus Christ, and allowing Him to maintain and bring forth that new nature which He put in us.

However, at the same time, we are still programmed to believe we continue to have the old sinful nature. The truth is, we no longer have the old nature, and we have the carryover from the old nature. What we have to do now is to eliminate the old habit patterns and old thought processes. We don't have to fight the old man anymore, the old man is dead. God did that in a supernatural way. God is the only one who can give life, so He made that transplantation inside us.

When we begin to understand all this, we can see that the reason we have low self-esteem is because we still think we have the old person inside us, pushing us to sin. That is a lie, because the old person is dead. The only thing we have pushing us to sin is the carryover from the influence of the old person. Satan would have us focus on the carryover, so he can bring us under condemnation because of the sin that remains in our lives.

But Jesus is revealing to us, "No, don't focus upon the sin that remains, simply focus upon Me." We must understand that focusing upon the carryover is focusing upon self, and that is exactly what satan wants us to do. But the Lord says, "Don't do that, focus on Me. I'll take care of that sinful nature. Just relax about that. If you will focus on Me, I will prove to you that I can wash you clean. I can really make you a new creation in Me."

We see that one undealt with emotion is a scab. What we have to do is lay down that emotion and cast our cares on the altar before the Lord and ask Him to consume it.

"Humble yourself under the mighty hand of God, and in due time He will exalt you. Casting all your cares on Him for He cares for you." (1 Peter 5:6-7)

As we continue to do this daily we will know who we are in Christ, and we can move on with Him. If we continue in our undealt with emotions, we will filter everything through them, and it will have an adverse effect upon everything we do.

Example: Low self-esteem generates self-consciousness. But self-consciousness is really "other's consciousness." Because we have a low opinion of ourselves, we are concerned about what other people may think about what we say or do. King Saul said, "I feared the people and listened to their voice." (1Samuel 15:19-24)

In many ways, we are like King Saul. Our concern for what others think creates inhibitions within us, and those inhibitions can cause us to miss God's perfect will for our lives. Because King Saul was more concerned with what the people thought than what God thought, he missed God's perfect will for his life. Like King Saul, we are going to be challenged constantly to compromise.

We must understand that if we give more attention to what people think and say about us, if we are more concerned about that, we may, in fact, miss God's perfect will for our lives.

It is never too late to change. It is never too late for God to do something worthwhile in our lives. God has the ability to accelerate healing, and to accelerate His purposes in a person's life. It is a mistake to think it is too late. We should never come to a point where we must say, "Oh well, what's the use." That will never be true, regardless of our age. It is never too late. When we believe that for ourselves, we can convey it to others.

The Importance of Setting Goals

Now let's consider the concept of establishing goals in our lives. We should accept the fact that no goal is worthwhile unless it glorifies God in some fashion. For this reason we need to take a long, hard look at our goals.

One of the problems we have as a society is what we will call the "I" Factor. The "I" Factor is when it's all about me; which means me first and all other things later. We have become an "I" society. Because of that, we have lost our ability to successfully meet our goals in life.

How backward we are when we get such a kick out of seeing a man win a million dollars in a lottery, but we resent the fellow who has worked all his life, invested properly and has accumulated a million dollars. Something is very wrong with a society like that. I phone, I pad, I pod, I, I, I!

The problem is the "I" Factor. We want what we want right now; we're not willing to discipline ourselves. For example, the "I" Factor says, "I'm not willing to wait on God. As a matter of fact, I'm not willing to wait on anything." The "I" Factor says, "I'm not going to wait until I can afford the television set, I'm going to go out and get the television set and charge it. I will pay that extra 18% finance charge because I want it now, and I'm going to get it now." But if someone suggests that we save 18% every week out of our pay check, we'll say, "What are you talking about, I can't save that much, I need that to live on!"

The "I" Factor says, "We've got to fulfill the great American dream, to have the largest house we can possibly afford." But, in reality, that is the great American nightmare, because we become financially locked into the house. Everything we do centers around that house. The money we pour into that house is absolutely incredible! We become in bondage to it, sacrificing our freedom to do and enjoy other things.

Why is it that the a person from another country comes to America, moves into a basement apartment, pays rent, and pretty soon he owns the entire city block? But the American who was born here can't even own his own home. The reason is the "I" Factor. The other person saves his money, he goes without, and invests wisely. But the American indulges in the "I" Factor, goes into debt and never gets out.

It all comes back to not being willing to wait on God to direct our steps. It simply takes too much time. We have developed a drive-through window mentality. We use the drive-through window, we pick up our order, and we eat it on the run. We pay more for it, and we know it isn't very healthy for us, but that's all right because it satisfies our need for "I want what I want and I want it now."

We have a tough day at work, so we come home and grab a beer out of the refrigerator. Why? Because we want to change our feeling, right now! It helps us to relax, immediately. It is the "I" Factor at work. That beer does its job so well we decide we'll have another. Then, before long, we have blown the whole evening, including our relationship with our family. It doesn't have to be beer, it could be marijuana, or any other mood-altering substance, or any sexual perversion.

We don't even consider the possibility of sitting down with our wives and saying, "I had kind of a tough time today. I'd like to tell you about it, and then I would appreciate it if you would pray for me." We are unwilling to wait for God to settle us down; we want relief, now! It's the "I" Factor at work.

The "I" Factor is a trap. Satan is riding hard on the "I" Factor in each of us. That very same trap has gotten most of the world into an incredible indebtedness. Some day we are going to have to pay for it, as a nation.

There is a way to escape that bondage. For example, if we will put to work for ourselves the process of compound interest, within 20 years we can be absolutely financially independent. This is how we can do it. From whatever we earn, we give 10% to God, and invest 10%, starting with a savings account. It doesn't make any difference how much we earn per week. We have been blowing that 20% all along.

If we will put it to work, in five years we will begin to see the curve that takes place when compound interest takes over. Depending upon how much we put in, we can shorten that to ten or fifteen years, but it is a guarantee that if we will do it for 20 years, each and every one of us can be financially independent. That means we will not be financially dependent upon anybody else, except Jesus.

Working towards financial independence can be a good goal. However, there are other good goals in life. We have been so accustomed to one way thinking, with all of our undealt with emotions that have caused addiction problems, and life controlling behaviors that we are not used to setting goals. We need help learning how to evaluate, set up and work toward healthy, godly goals for our lives.

Our goals can now be established from a basis of a healthy self-esteem, since we are learning to identify with Christ. He will help us reach for goals of ministering to Him and to others. He will help us walk toward Him and His desire for us, in faith, hope and love.

The majority of people have no idea how to go about establishing goals. It is all right to establish goals, then to continue to adjust them as our situations change. That is a healthy approach to goal setting.

1. What five things do I value most in life?

2. What are my three most important goals right now?

3. If I won a million dollars in a lottery, how would I spend it? List 4 ways, with no limitations.

4. How would you spend your time if you knew you had only three months to live?

5. What have I always wanted to do, but been afraid to try?

6. Of all the things I have done, what has given me the greatest feeling of im-portance or success? (This could be my area of excellence)

7.   If I had one wish which would enable me to accomplish whatever I want, what would that be, if I knew absolutely that I could not fail?

8.   Pick one major goal to commit all your energies and efforts to achieve. The goal is:

9.   Next, list three to six activities necessary to start working on and accomplish your goal.

10. List three to six actions necessary to accomplish each of the activities.

Finally, prioritize each of the six actions and schedule them in a monthly plan book with specific days, along with the time on those days that you will implement each action.

This should be a helpful process through which we can arrive at our primary goal in life. It would be wise to take time and consider this. We must remember we are new creatures in Christ. And we must also remember Christ must be in the goal. That doesn't mean the goal has to be a super spiritual goal, it just means that Christ must be the center in everything we do.

A word about prosperity—we can't handle it on our own. If we will study the nation of Israel, we will see they could never handle God's prosperity. They always took their eyes off God and put their eyes on material things. In every case, it wasn't very long before they were back in bondage to another nation.

Prosperity can be very deceptive. In the majority of cases, if we approach a wealthy person and tell him he needs Jesus Christ, he may well reply, "Why do I need Jesus Christ? I have everything I need." He feels no need for Jesus Christ. There will come a time in our lives, if we keep our eyes focused upon Jesus Christ, that He will, in fact, exalt us. That will probably be the biggest test in our lives, because we have a tendency, a natural tendency, especially if we have had low self-esteem, to take the prosperity God is giving us, and become puffed up like a rooster. But it won't be long before something or someone chops off our head!

The more material things we have and the more success we experience, the less time we tend to spend with God. Possessions have a tendency to possess us. The man who has a million dollars is very concerned about keeping the million dollars. He is so concerned that he puts all his energies and efforts upon keeping the million dollars. He tries to get another million just so he can protect the first million. And many times God is left out in the process.

Some of us will do as suggested here, keeping Jesus as the center all the way through. If so, it is a principle that He will, in all probability, prosper us in some fashion. If so, we should never forget where that prosperity came from. We should never think we have it all figured out, and that we can handle whatever comes our way. The fact is, as soon as we think we are in charge, we are no longer in charge. The Prince of the Power of the Air will come in to persuade, guide and direct us, and the result will be disaster. So, our acid test may come in the form of prosperity. It may be easy to look to God when we are down, but when we are on top of the world, that is a different story.

Many of us get healed from toxic and damaged emotions, but still try to get our love, joy, peace, and happiness from the current world system. We come out of deep addiction and receive healing on the inside and then say to ourselves, "If I can just get a great job, wife, kids back, home, car and friends then all will be well."

We must never forget that many of us have had all of these things yet they were not enough to keep us happy. Our love, joy, peace, and happiness have to come daily by meeting with the Lord; talking to Him and letting Him talk to us.

The goal exercise we just participated in, takes us beyond simply getting healed from life controlling type issues like drugs, sex, food and alcohol. It takes us into another dimension. We must keep in mind that we have to take Jesus Christ with us into that next dimension, daily. We are back in the flesh and headed toward the old life if we don't.

It has been said that true healing is not a manipulation of the current situation; it is a change of heart. It is not brought on by a change of circumstances, even though a change of circumstances may accompany it. As we discover who we are in Christ, our goals for this life will adequately reflect His heart.

Questions

1. Why is an undealt with emotion a scab that must become a scar?

2. Why do we continue to sin even though we have a new nature incapable of sin?

3. How do we decrease in order for the Holy Spirit to increase within us?

4. Why is it important for us not to be overly sensitive of what others think and say about us?

5.   In what ways does the "I" Factor work against our relationship with God?

6.   Why is it Important to have Christ at the center of our goals and part of His will?

session thirteen

PURPOSE

As we come to the final session of walking you through soul healing, we have had many opportunities to revisit some painful experiences from our past. Hopefully, God has begun a major healing process in you.

In the midst of our life controlling behaviors, the majority of us didn't take the time to examine our lives with the intention of identifying our goals or to look for any purpose in living. The reason for this session is to look back upon our lives and see clearly how our motives, values, goals, and purposes have been focused in the wrong direction. We will see how this has caused us painful and frustrating experiences.

We will also look at God's purpose for our lives, and how to live that purpose on a daily basis. There are four major areas surrounding the subject of purpose. We will approach them from a Biblical viewpoint as well as from a relational aspect.

Purpose of the Current World System

"And He told them a parable, saying, 'The land of a certain rich man was very productive.' And he began reasoning to himself, saying, 'What shall I do, since I have no place to store my crops?' And he said, 'This is what I will do: I will tear down my barns and build larger ones, and there I will store all my grain and my goods,' and I will say to my soul, 'Soul, you have many goods laid up for many years to come; take your ease, eat, drink and be merry.' But God said to him, 'You fool! This very night your soul is required of you; and now who will own what you have prepared?' So is the man who lays up treasure for himself, and is not rich toward God." Luke 12:16-21

Most of us have had the same problem as the rich man. Our purpose in life has been to accumulate enough wealth to be able to take it easy as soon as possible for the rest of our lives. That is the reason so many people play the lottery.

All our energies have been focused upon money, alcohol, drugs, sex, power, and every kind of materialistic toy that promises to make life easier and more fun. We spend our entire lives striving to achieve success in the world. We never come to the realization, like the rich man, that our purpose for life, even though successful in the world's eyes, has been a failure in the eyes of God.

We are similar to the man who climbed the ladder of success and, after many years of hard work, reached the top, only to discover that the ladder was leaning against the wrong building.

Like the rich man, we who live for the wrong purpose in life don't time for God. What has actually happened is that our purpose for life has become our god. When our belief system in life is wrong because we don't include God, our behavior will also be wrong.

No Purpose

> "As a result, we are no longer to be children, tossed here and there by waves, and carried about by every wind of doctrine, by the trickery of men, by craftiness in deceitful scheming." Ephesians 4:14 GNT

The most common saying of people who live with no purpose in life is, "If it feels good, do it."

Many of us who have been heavily into drugs, alcohol, and sex at one time may have lost hope, existing only under the medication of our addiction, with no purpose for our lives. We were as the Scripture states, "tossed to and fro." We did whatever made us feel good.

Transients and other street people are examples of those who live with no purpose for their lives. Another is a person who gives up completely, and takes his own life.

Generally speaking, the profile of a person who lives with no purpose in life is one who has no belief in God, and behaves as he wants to behave, regardless of the consequences.

Mixed Purposes

> "No one can serve two masters; for either he will hate the one and love the other, or he will hold to one and despise the other. You cannot serve God and money." Matthew 6:24

> "You cannot drink the cup of the Lord and the cup of demons; you cannot partake of the table of the Lord and the table of demons." I Corinthians 10:21

Living our lives in mixed purposes produces misery. A man caught up in a mixed purpose believes in God, but he lives a hellish life. He grasps at God with one hand while his other hand holds onto certain vices he continues to enjoy in life.

It has been said that such a man howls with the wolves on Saturday night and bleats with the sheep on Sunday morning. It is impossible for him to be at peace in either place. As the Scripture says that man is trying to serve two masters. And that is an impossible task.

God's Purpose

"But seek first His kingdom and His righteousness; and all these things shall be added to you." Matthew 6:33

The man who lives with a right purpose is, first of all, a man who has a close personal relationship with God. God is number one in his life. Because of this, God is able to work in him both to will and to work for His good pleasure.

God's purpose for us is revealed throughout the Scriptures. Simply put, we were created to commune with Him and to receive and give His love. We are examples to others of His grace and love because He has chosen to impart His life and His righteousness to vessels as faulty as ours.

As we seek His kingdom first, we realize He is mainly interested in loving His creation. As we allow Him to use us to love others with His love we fulfill our greatest call, and bring honor and praise to God.

When we are living in the right purpose, God is able to bring healing and restoration into our lives. Our motives, values and goals in life will conform to His purpose for us. As a result, we experience the soul (mind, will, and emotions) peace and security for which we have been searching.

The man with a right purpose has a Godly belief system, and his behavior conforms to his Godly beliefs. He not only thinks right, he lives life right according to the plans God has for him.

1. Why is it important for me to examine my life and to look for a purpose to live?

2. Why is it a wrong purpose to want to accumulate wealth in order to live an easy life?

3. What is wrong with the concept, "If it feels good, do it?"

4. Why is it impossible to serve both God and money?

The goal of this workbook is for you to read it fully, one to two times to get a clear understanding of how you became addicted and afflicted. Then find someone who can help walk you through the Inner Healing Process. If you do not have anyone that can help you with this, we do offer through our Counseling Center, the ability for you to call and receive counseling with us over the phone, via skype, or in the office.

Look us up on our book website www.addictednomore.org and click counseling tab and then click in the middle of the page and you will come to this website www.jasonmillercounselingcenter.com

PRAYERS FOR HEALING

Forgiving What Others Have Done To Me Prayer*

Father, I know your will for my life is to forgive others in the same manner you forgave me, yet my soul (mind, will, and emotions) has been fighting it. Without your help, I do not have the ability to forgive anyone. Therefore, I am coming to you and asking in the name of Jesus, to fill my entire soul and physical body with your forgiveness and love. Lord Jesus, as Your forgiveness and love fills me, I ask you to help me to have the willingness to forgive (say the name of who you need to forgive) for (name the thing they did that hurt you), the same way you have forgiven me for all my sins. In the name of Jesus I choose right now to forgive _____. Father, I repent and ask You to forgive me for having an unforgiving heart, for holding anger, bitterness, grudges, and judgments against _____ and I, at this very minute release _____ and give him/her to you. Lord, I cancel the assignment of unforgiveness towards _____ and chose to release _____ from this day forward and forever with Your help. Thank You Lord.

Forgiving What I've Done To Others Prayer

Lord, as I look over my life, I see that out of my hurt, pain, anger, depression, and failed attempt to deal with my emotions and fill the empty void, I have caused these same feelings in others. I confess that the guilt and shame for how I treated others have added to my pain and hurt. So Father I'm asking You to forgive me for what I said and done (name what you said and or done) to (name of the person). Lord, I call these things sin against them and You. Father, I ask that You take the emotional and/or physical harm away from _____ caused by what I did. Remove the guilt and shame I feel for doing these things to_____. I also ask for an open door, if it be Your will, to personally ask forgiveness to _____ and to make amends if money is involved by attempting to do the best I can to repay. Lord, I release them from the pain it has caused both them and me. Thank You for restoring me as if I never committed these sins against anyone.

Soul Tie Prayer*

Father, in the name and authority of the Lord Jesus Christ, I renounce, give up, cast off, and sever the unhealthy and unholy sexual Soul Tie with (name of the person). I call back to myself every part of my mind, will, and emotions that is attached to me to come back to me, from _____ and I send back to _____ all their mind, will, and emotions that was attached to them from being in a unhealthy sexual soul tie with me. I ask You to erase from both of us every ungodly feeling, desire, imagination, trauma, pain, hurt, anger or thought that we both have in our souls all the way down to the smallest memory.

(After you've gone through this prayer with each person, finalize with this prayer with the following:)

In the power and authority of the name of the Lord Jesus, I break every yoke of bondage and I command every unclean spirit attached to these ungodly soul ties to go from my life right now, causing no harm to me or my family and place them under the feet of Jesus Christ, never to return again. Holy Spirit, cleanse me and fill me with God's love, joy, peace, purity, and healing presence in all the empty places where the unclean spirits formerly resided and seal me with blood of Jesus. Thank You Lord for restoring my Soul.

Forgiving My Self Prayer

Father, the hardest thing I for me to do is to forgive myself. Now I understand that was not the real me that did these things to others and myself. It was me attempting to deal with my Soul (mind, will, and emotions) without You and trying to reconnect the empty void that happened in the Garden when Adam and Eve sinned. I have cleaned up my soul through visiting each incident and receiving healing and have invited Jesus to come and live in my Empty Void which is my Spirit, the New Me.

Today I speak to myself, letting myself of the hook, choosing to forgive myself and restoring myself to a mighty Son of God perfect in God's sight. I confess that if God does not remember my sins and faults and the hurts and pains I have caused others, neither do I (Is 43:25). I have asked for forgiveness and God's Word says in 1 John 1:9 that if we confess our sins that He is faithful and just to cleanse us from all unrighteousness (guilt, shame, and unforgiveness towards self). Thank You, Lord, for allowing me to forgive myself. I confess and renounce all shame and guilt from my past, never to remember it again, and cast and rebuke every negative spirit that was attached to me from the guilt and shame, and command them to never come back. In the name of Jesus I seal myself in my new spirit man as a New Creation in Christ- never to go back to the old me, in the name of Jesus.

My New Life with Christ Confession Prayer*

My confession over my life according to the Word of God is as follows:

I will, starting this day with help of God, love others with genuine affection and take delight in honoring others. I will hate only what is wrong and hold tightly to what is right and good. I will work hard and try my best to serve My Lord with joy. I have confidence in my hope and thank God that my name is written in Heaven's book and never be removed. I declare that I will be patience in impatience situations; I will practice being nice, caring and giving to others; I will not pay back evil for evil and I will bless and pray that God blesses those who persecute me and those who spitefully use me, understanding that I use to be that way. My thoughts and actions will be honorable and I will do the right thing even when no one is looking. I will do my best to keep company with anyone set before me and live in peace with everyone.

I will choose daily to forgive, not storing any negative emotions into my soul, following Jesus' example to love and forgive. The result of my walking in love and forgiveness will produce the fruits of the Holy Spirit: love, joy, peace, patience, kindness, goodness, faithfulness, gentleness, and self-control in my life. I will walk in and pursue God's kind of love. I am patience, kind, not jealous, not boastful, not proud, nor rude. I don't demand my own way and I am not easily angered. I don't keep any record of when I've been wronged. I believe the best about people. My love protects, trusts, hopes, perseveres, and does not fail.

I will love the Lord my God with all my heart, soul, mind, and strength. I humble myself under the mighty power of God, and at the right time He will lift me up in honor. I will take full responsibility for all my actions. I am not selfish and I don't need to impress people. I will not just look out for my own interests but for the interests of others. I will have the mind of Christ and will aim to live in such a way that reveals this.

All the words that come out of my mouth are truthful. I don't lie because God has stripped me of my old sinful nature and all its wicked deeds and has put on me a new nature. My mind is renewed daily as I learn to know my Creator and become like Him. I choose to take every thought captive to the obedience of Christ and deal with these thoughts so as to never store a negative thought in my emotions.

My body belongs to the Lord Jesus who bought it with His precious blood. My body is the temple of the Holy Spirit and I will respect and take good care of it by having healthy eating habits. I have a passion and respect for the sanctity of life because You made each person by your own hands. You, God, ordained and sustained marriages and I believe the sanctity of marriage being between a man and a women.

Thank you for my new life. I commit to meet with you daily to share my thoughts and emotions, both positive and negative. I commit to letting You share with me daily Your thoughts and emotions with me. I love You, my Lord, and am so proud to be called your son (or daughter). I love You!

Permission to use from ECCC in my own words

REFERENCES

Session I

(Philippians 3:12-14 NKJV), "Not that I have already attained, or am already perfected; but I press on, that I may lay hold of that for which Christ Jesus has laid hold of me. Brothers I do not count myself to have apprehended; but one thing I do, forgetting those things which are behind and reaching forward to those things ahead, I press toward the goal for the prize of the upward call of God in Christ Jesus."

When the Lord got Saul's (who was later named Paul's) attention on the road to Damascus. (Acts 9)

Jesus says in the Bible, "Are you tired or (weary)? Worn out? Burned out on religion? Come to me. Get away with me and you will recover your life (and find rest in your soul). I'll show you how to take a real rest (in your soul). Walk with me and work with me-watch how I do it. Learn the unforced rhythms of grace (unmerited favor). I won't put anything heavy (laden) or ill-fitting on you. Keep Company with me and you'll learn freely and lightly."(Matthew 11:28-30 MSG, NKJV)

Session 2

(Psalm 139:13-16 MSG): "Oh yes, you shaped me first inside, then out; you formed me in my mother's womb. I thank you High GodYou're breathtaking! Body and soul, I am marvelously made! I worship in adoration-what a creation! You know me inside out, you know my every bone in my body, and you know exactly how I was made, bit by bit, how I was sculpted from nothing into something. Like an open book, you watched me grow from conception to birth; all the stages of my life were spread out before you, the days of my life all prepared before I'd even lived one day."

The Bible says, "For if you forgive others for their faults, your heavenly Father will also forgive you. But if you do not forgive others, then your heavenly Father will not forgive your faults." (Matthew 6:14-15GW)

Session 3

The Bible talks about how damaged emotions affect us, here are a few examples.

(Proverbs 15:13 NASB) "A joyful heart makes a cheerful face, but when the heart is sad, the spirit is broken." (One of the products of rejection is a broken spirit.)

(Proverbs 17:22 NASB) "A joyful heart is good medicine, but a broken spirit dries up the bones." (A broken spirit, brought about by rejection is capable of drying up, or taking away the desire for life.)

(Proverbs 18:14 NASB) "The spirit of a man can endure his sickness, but a broken spirit who can bear?" (If the desire for life has gone, there is no chance for healing to take place.)

Even Jesus Himself was despised and rejected a man of sorrows and acquainted with deepest grief. See Isaiah 53; this whole chapter paints a picture of the Lord understanding what we are going through because He went through it, so He is able to help us through it because He loves us and endured these emotions that we may be free of them.

The most powerful positive emotional force in the universe is the love of God, (1 John 4:8,16 NASB) "The one who does not love does not know God, for God is love. And we have come to know and have believed the love which God has for us. God is love and the one who abides in love abides in God, God abides in him, and he in God." God is love; therefore, love is God's most powerful force.

Session 5

But we now have God, and God tells us He wants us to cast all our cares on Him for He cares for us. (1 Peter 5:7)

(Matthew 14:13 NLT): "Now when Jesus heard it, He withdrew from there in a boat to a lonely place by Himself..." Jesus went to a place where He could be alone to grieve for John the Baptist who had been beheaded by Herod.

(John 11:33-36 NIV): "When Jesus therefore saw her weeping, and the Jews who came with her, also weeping, He was deeply moved in spirit, and was troubled, and said, 'Where have you laid him?' They said to Him, 'Lord, come and see.' Jesus wept. And so the Jews were saying, 'Behold how He loved him'" Jesus wept at the tomb of Lazarus, for He was grieved in His spirit.

Session 6

What Jesus said about forgiveness, (Matthew 18:21-35): "At that point Peter got up the nerve to ask, 'Master, how many times do I forgive a brother or sister who hurts me? Seven?' Jesus replied, 'Seven!' Hardly. Try seventy times seven. The kingdom of God is like a king who decided to settle his accounts with his servant. As he got under way, one servant was brought before him who owed a debt of a hundred thousand dollars.

He couldn't pay up, so the king ordered the man, along with his wife, children, and goods, to be auctioned off at the slave market. The servant threw himself at the king's feet and begged, 'Give me a chance and I'll pay it all back.' Touched by his plea, the king let him off, erasing the entire debt.

The servant was no sooner out of the room when he came upon one of his fellow servants who owed him ten dollars. He seized him by the throat and demanded, 'Pay up, now!' The servant threw himself down and begged, 'Give me a chance and I'll pay it back.' But he wouldn't do it. He had him arrested and put in jail until the debt was paid.

When the other servants saw this going on, they were outraged and brought a detailed report to the king. "The king summoned the man and said, 'You evil servant! I forgave your entire debt when you begged for mercy. Shouldn't you be compelled to be merciful to your fellow servant who asked for mercy?'

And his king, moved with anger handed him over to the tortures until he should repay all that was owed him.

So shall my heavenly Father also do to you, if each of you does not forgive his brother or sister from your heart?" (MSG and KJV Bibles)

James 5:16a: "Therefore confess your sins to one another and pray for one another, so that you may be healed."

Sin is unexplainable and Paul in the Bible even said, "The things I do I do not understand." (Romans 7:15)

It states in the Bible that we are to "Give all you worries and cares to God, for he cares about you." (1 Peter 5:7 NLT)

Our reaction to our perceived mistreatment may have caused us to treat others the same way we were treated. We may have been filled with anger, hurt and hatred. We may have even committed murder, if not actually, in our hearts. (1 John 3:15); (Matthew 5:21-26)

(Ephesians 4:32 ESV): "And be kind to one another, tender-hearted, forgiving each other, just as God in Christ also has forgiven you."

"If we confess our sins, He is faithful and just to forgive us our sins and to cleanse us from all unrighteousness." (1 John 1:9 NKJV

"...You are truly my disciples if you remain faithful to my teachings. And you will know the truth, and the truth will set you free."(John 8:32)

Session 7

Jesus said in the book of John that He would give us peace. Not the peace that the world would give to us, but His peace (John 14:27). That is what makes us whole and healthy.

John 18:15-27 Living Bible (TLB)

John 21:3-17 New Living Translation (NLT)

Session 8

"Do not judge others, and you will not be judged. For you will be treated as you treat others." The standard you use in judging others is the standard by which you will be judged. (Matthew 7: 1-2)

"Therefore, you are without excuse, every one of you who passes judgment, for in that you judge another, you condemn yourself; for you who judge practice the same things." (Romans 2:1 NASB)

"Don't be deceived, God is not mocked; for whatever a man sows, this he will also reap."(Galatians 6:7 NASB)

Session 9

"For this cause a man shall leave his father and mother, and shall cleave to his wife; and the two shall become one flesh." (Ephesians 5:31 NASB) A husband and wife are bonded together by love.

"Consequently they are no longer two, but one flesh. What therefore God has joined together let no man separate." (Matthew 19:6 NASB)

"Now it came about when he had finished speaking to Saul that the soul of Jonathan was knit to the soul of David, and Jonathan loves him as himself." (1 Samuel 18:1 NASB)

"A man of many friends comes to ruin, but there is a friend who sticks closer than a brother."(Proverbs 18:24 NASB)

"Now, therefore when I come to your servant my father and the lad is not with us, since his life is bound up in the lad's life (his soul knitted with the lad's soul), it will come about when he sees that the lad is not with us, that he will die…" (Genesis 44:30-31 NASB, parenthesis mine)

Christian soul ties are as if "from the whole body, being fitted and held together by every joint supplies, according to the proper working of each individual part, causes the growth of the body for the building up of itself in love." (Ephesians 4:16 NASB)

"Or do you not know that one who joins himself to a harlot is one body with her. For He says, the two will become one flesh," (1 Corinthians 6:16 NASB)

"For they exchanged the truth of God for a lie, and worshipped and served the creature (satan) rather than the Creator, Who is blessed forever. Amen. For this cause God gave them over to degrading passions; for even their women did change the natural use into that which is against nature itself: And likewise also men, leaving the natural use of woman, burned in their lust toward another; men with men working that which is unseemly, and receive in themselves the due penalty of their error." (Romans 1:25-27 NASB)

Confessing each one out loud releases it from your soul and we are doing what the Bible says in James 5:16, to confess your faults one to another and pray for each other so that you may be healed.

Session 10

"For I was born a sinner-yes, from the moment my mother conceived me." (Psalm 51:5 NLT) "When Adam sinned, sin entered the world. Adam's sin brought death (to our souls), so death spread to everyone, for everyone sins." (Romans 5:12 NLT)

We can see through the Bible that Job felt this way about what happened to him. "For He (God) is not a man as I am that I may answer Him, that we may go to court together, if there was only a mediator between us, who could bring us together." (Job 9:32-33 NKJV)

"Therefore the Lord Himself will give you a sign: Behold, a virgin will be with child and bear a son, and she will call His name Immanuel (which means God with us)." (Isaiah 7:14 NIV)

About 800 years before Jesus was born, God revealed His forthcoming birth through prophet's writing prophecies that came true in. (Matthew 1:21-25)

The Apostle Paul actually came to a level of maturity where he could rejoice in his infirmities, because God could manifest His strength in Paul's weaknesses. (2 Corinthians 12:10)

"And she gave birth to her firstborn, a son; and she wrapped him in cloths, and placed him in a manger, because there was no guest room available for them." (Luke 2:7 NIV)

"No one of illegitimate birth shall enter the assembly of the Lord, none of his descendants, even to the tenth generation, shall enter the assembly of the Lord." Jesus also experienced generational curses. The strongest curse in the Old Testament is found in this verse. (Deuteronomy 23:2 NKJV)

"And so they were saying to Him, 'Where is Your Father?' Jesus answered, 'You know neither Me, nor My Father; if you knew Me, you would know My Father also.' The Pharisees are saying, 'You, who have no father, who are you to tell us about our father? Our father was Abraham.'" But Jesus responded by telling them their father was the "father of lies," the devil. (John 8:19 NKJV)

"Christ redeemed us from the curse of the law, having become a curse for us—for it is written, 'Cursed is everyone who hangs on a Tree...'" (Galatians 3:13 NKJV)

"Since therefore the children share in flesh and blood, he himself likewise partook of the same things, that through death he might destroy the one who has the power of death, that is, the devil, and deliver all those who through fear of death were subject to lifelong slavery. for surely it is not angels that he helps, but he helps the offspring of Abraham. Therefore he had to be made like his brothers in every respect, so that he might become a merciful and faithful high priest in the service of God, to make propitiation for the sins of the people. For because he himself has suffered when tempted, he is able to help those who are being tempted." (Hebrews 2:14-18 ESV)

These verses show us Jesus also identified with our temptations. The Bible says He was tempted in all points. We have no reason to remain sick or wounded any longer.

Jesus is able to help us because of what He accomplished. 1 Corinthians 10:13 tells us there is no temptation which is not common to man. When that temptation comes, God will provide a way of escape. James said, "Blessed is the man who endures temptation, for after he has been tested, he will receive the crown of life." If He says we can endure it, we can endure it, because the power of Jesus Christ comes into us to identify with us.

"Since then we have a great high priest who has passed through the heavens, Jesus the Son of God, let us hold fast our confession. For we do not have a high priest who cannot sympathize with our weaknesses, but one who has been tempted in all things as we are, yet without sin. Let us therefore draw near with confidence to the throne of grace that we may receive mercy and may find grace to help in time of need." (Hebrews 4:14-16 ESV)

Isaiah 53 tells us Jesus was despised and rejected; He was a man of sorrows (pains); He was acquainted with grief (sicknesses); He was wounded for our transgressions; He was bruised for our iniquities; the chastisement of our peace was upon Him, and by His stripes (lashes), we are (have been) healed. (Isaiah 53:3-5)

The Bible says that Jesus is the last Adam. He came to restore and to recover what the first Adam lost. The first thing He encountered as He started His ministry was the wilderness experience with the devil. He faced three temptations in the wilderness (Matthew 4:1-11). It is interesting that we can find three similar temptations in the Garden of Eden. (Genesis 3:1-7)

Jesus tells us that He knows we have been rejected, so he wants to take our rejection from us and give us His acceptance. Hear Him say, "I want to take your sense of unworthiness from you and give you of My worth." (Isaiah 53:3-5)

"I have been crucified with Christ; and it is no longer I who live, but Christ lives in me; and the life which I now live in the flesh I live by faith in the Son of God, who loved me, and delivered Himself up for me." (Galatians 2:20 ESV)

"And when you were dead in your transgressions and the uncircumcision of your flesh, He made you alive together with Him, having forgiven us all our transgressions, having canceled out the certificate of debt consisting of decrees against us and which was hostile to us; and He has taken it out of the way, having nailed it to the cross." (Colossians 2:13-14 NASB)

"In Him, you also, after listening to the message of truth, the gospel of your salvation–having also believed, you were sealed in Him with the Holy Spirit of promise, who is given as a pledge of our inheritance, with a view to the redemption of God's own possession, to the praise of His glory." (Ephesians 1:13-14 NASB)

Session 11

"And do not be conformed to this world, but be transformed by the renewing of your mind, that you may prove what the will of God is, that which is good and acceptable and perfect." (Romans 12:2 NASB)

"Therefore, holy brethren, partakers of a heavenly calling, consider Jesus, the Apostle and High Priest of our confession." (Hebrews 3:1 NASB)

"Now the main point in what has been said is this: we have such a High Priest, who has taken His seat at the right hand of the throne of the majesty in the heavens, a minister in the sanctuary, and in the true tabernacle, which the Lord pitched, not man. For every High Priest appointed to offer both gifts and sacrifices; hence it is necessary that this High Priest also have something to offer." (Hebrews 8:1-3 NASB)

Session 12

Inside us is a spirit being which contains the Spirit of Christ, and the Spirit of Christ is incapable of sin (2 Corinthians 5:17). We have within us this spirit person, this new being, this new birth, which says, "I am incapable of sin, and I will not sin. There is no way in the world I am going to sin."

However, at the same time, we are still programmed to believe we continue to have the old sinful nature. The truth is, we no longer have the old nature, and we have the carryover from the old nature. What we have to do now is to eliminate the old habit patterns and old thought processes. We don't have to fight the old man anymore, the old man is dead. God did that in a supernatural way. God is the only one who can give life, so He made that transplantation inside us. Study Romans 6, and Galatians 2.

John the Baptist didn't say, "I must decrease, that He may increase." He said, "He must increase, but I must decrease." (John 3:30 NASB)

"Humble yourself under the mighty hand of God, that He may life you up in due time. Casting all your anxiety on Him for He cares for you." (1 Peter 5:6-7 NIV)

Saul said that he feared the people and listened to their voice.

(1 Sam 15:19-24)

Session 13

"And He told them a parable, saying, 'The land of a certain rich man was very productive. And he began reasoning to himself, saying, 'What shall I do, since I have no place to store my crops?' And he said, 'This is what I will do: I will tear down my barns and build larger ones, and there I will store all my grain and my goods, and I will say to my soul, soul, you have many goods laid up for many years to come; take your ease, eat, drink and be merry.' But God said to him, 'You fool! This very night your soul is required of you; and now who will own what you have prepared?' So is the man who lays up treasure for himself, and is not rich toward God." (Luke 12:16-21 NASB)

"As a result, we are no longer to be children, tossed here and there by waves, and carried about by every wind of doctrine, by the trickery of men, by craftiness in deceitful scheming." (Ephesians 4:14 NASB)

"No one can serve two masters; for either he will hate the one and love the other, or he will hold to one and despise the other. You cannot serve God and money." (Matthew 6:24 NIV)

"You cannot drink the cup of the Lord and the cup of demons; you cannot partake of the table of the Lord and the table of demons."
(1 Corinthians 10:21 ESV)

"But seek first His kingdom and His righteousness; and all these things will be give to you as well." (Matthew 6:33 NIV) See also Ephesians 1:4-12 and Ephesians 3:6-21 for further study on purpose.

Made in the USA
San Bernardino, CA
01 August 2020